A FINE WILL BE CHARGED
FOR EACH OVERDUE BOOK

POETRY & LIFE

COLERIDGE & HIS POETRY

AMS PRESS
NEW YORK

Samuel Taylor Coleridge

COLERIDGE & HIS POETRY

BY

KATHLEEN E. ROYDS

LONDON: GEORGE G.
HARRAP & COMPANY
9 PORTSMOUTH STREET
KINGSWAY W.C. ✦ MCMXII

One volume of the Poetry and Life Series
published by AMS Press

Reprinted by special arrangement with
George G. Harrap & Co. Ltd., London

From the edition of 1912, London

First AMS edition published in 1971

Manufactured in the United States of America

International Standard Book Number:
Complete Set: 0-404-52500-8
This Volume: 0-404-52532-6

Library of Congress Catalog Card Number: 76-120990

AMS PRESS INC.
NEW YORK, N.Y. 10003

GENERAL PREFACE

A GLANCE through the pages of this little book will suffice to disclose the general plan of the series of which it forms a part. Only a few words of explanation, therefore, will be necessary.

The point of departure is the undeniable fact that with the vast majority of young students of literature a living interest in the work of any poet can best be aroused, and an intelligent appreciation of it secured, when it is immediately associated with the character and career of the poet himself. The cases are indeed few and far between in which much fresh light will not be thrown upon a poem by some knowledge of the personality of the writer, while it will often be found that the most direct—perhaps even the only—way to the heart of its meaning lies through a consideration of the circumstances in which it had its birth. The purely æsthetic critic may possibly object that a poem should be regarded simply as a self-contained and detached piece of art, having no personal affiliations or bearings. Of the validity of this as an abstract principle nothing need now be said. The fact remains that, in the earlier stages of study at any rate, poetry is most valued and loved when it is made to seem most human and vital ; and the human and vital interest of poetry can be most surely brought home to the reader by the biographical method of interpretation.

5

GENERAL PREFACE

This is to some extent recognised by writers of histories and text-books of literature, and by editors of selections from the works of our poets ; for place is always given by them to a certain amount of biographical material. But in the histories and text-books the biography of a given writer stands by itself, and his work has to be sought elsewhere, the student being left to make the connection for himself ; while even in our current editions of selections there is little systematic attempt to link biography, step by step, with production.

This brings us at once to the chief purpose of the present series. In this, biography and production will be considered together and in intimate association. In other words, an endeavour will be made to interest the reader in the lives and personalities of the poets dealt with, and at the same time to use biography as an introduction and key to their writings.

Each volume will therefore contain the life-story of the poet who forms its subject. In this, attention will be specially directed to his personality as it expressed itself in his poetry, and to the influences and conditions which counted most as formative factors in the growth of his genius. This biographical study will be used as a setting for a selection, as large as space will permit, of his representative poems. Such poems, where possible, will be reproduced in full, and care will be taken to bring out their connection with his character, his circumstances, and the movement of his mind. Then, in

GENERAL PREFACE

addition, so much more general literary criticism will be incorporated as may seem to be needed to supplement the biographical material, and to exhibit both the essential qualities and the historical importance of his work.

It is believed that the plan thus pursued is substantially in the nature of a new departure, and that the volumes of this series, constituting as they will an introduction to the study of some of our greatest poets, will be found useful to teachers and students of literature, and no less to the general lover of English poetry.

WILLIAM HENRY HUDSON

POEMS QUOTED IN WHOLE OR IN PART

COLERIDGE AND HIS POETRY

SAMUEL TAYLOR COLERIDGE was born in the little Devonshire town of Ottery St. Mary, on October 21, 1772. His father, vicar of the parish and chaplain-priest and master of its Free Grammar School, had married twice, and Coleridge was the youngest of a family of nine sons and one daughter, children of his second marriage.

His mother was a woman eminently practical and of strong common sense, anxious " to make gentlemen of her sons "—a task which her un-worldly, visionary husband was quite content to leave in her hands. But the Rev. John Coleridge recognised the remarkable ability of his youngest son. He took him for long walks and talked to him on subjects in which he himself was interested, and he early decided that this son should follow his footsteps and enter the Church.

In the character of his father may be found many traits which afterwards came out, accentuated and developed, in Coleridge himself. John Coleridge was the son of a woollen trader of South Molton. On his father's failure in business he had been turned out penniless to make his own way. A lover of learning, he managed to get to Cambridge, where he became a sound Greek, Latin, and Hebrew scholar and a mathematician ; he took Orders, and finally obtained the Vicarage of Ottery St. Mary. Here, as vicar and schoolmaster, he gained a reputation for naïve eccentricity, for lovable simplicity, and for absent-mindedness. That they might hear the actual words of the Holy Spirit, he would quote Hebrew to his marvelling congregation ; or, for the benefit of his pupils' mothers, explain with length and learning why he proposed, in his Latin Grammar, to substitute the name " quale-quare-quidditive " by way of simplification, for the term " ablative." Coleridge always revered his memory as that indeed of " an Israelite without guile."

The best impression of Coleridge's character as a child is given us by himself in letters written some years after to one of the staunchest of his many staunch friends, Thomas Poole, of Nether Stowey. When due allowance has been made for the idealising tendency common in looking back on childhood, and especially so, perhaps, in those highly endowed with poetic powers, the picture that stands out is that of a remarkable child, solitary, imaginative, and precocious. Driven by childish jealousy of a favoured brother to seek refuge in himself, he " took no pleasure in boyish sports but read incessantly." " So," he adds, thus significantly early, " I became a dreamer." " Robinson Crusoe " he read before the age of six, and the " Arabian Nights' Entertainments," which came soon after, so excited his imagination that his father had his books taken away from him.

COLERIDGE & HIS POETRY

One story he tells of an early adventure, which has its significance in its after-effects. Fearing a whipping after a quarrel with a brother, to escape punishment he ran away from home one evening, and spent the whole night on the bank of the Otter, waking to find himself thoroughly chilled and unable to walk. A severe illness followed, and here was, perhaps, the beginning of that ill-health, partly inherited, which was destined to dog his footsteps throughout his life.

From six to nine he was educated at the Grammar School, where, he says, " I . . . soon outstripped all of my age." But when he was nine years old his father died suddenly ; early the next year an old pupil at the Grammar School managed to get him a presentation for Christ's Hospital. Thus, a mere child, he left Ottery and its early, home influences, only to come to it again as an occasional visitor, and that not till " many various-fated years " had passed.

On arriving in London Coleridge stayed for some weeks with an uncle on his mother's side, who kept a tobacconist's shop in the City. He was very proud of his precocious nephew and very unwise, if we may judge from Coleridge's recollections, in the way he showed his admiration. He used, Coleridge says, " to carry me from coffee-house to coffee-house and tavern to tavern, where I drank and talked and disputed, as if I had been a man." After six weeks at the preparatory school at Hertford, Coleridge was moved, in September 1782, to Christ's

Hospital, to pass soon into the Upper School, under the tutelage of the Rev. T. Boyer—a promotion, it is said, which followed on the report of a senior boy who found him reading Virgil for his own pleasure.

Of the state of things at Christ's Hospital at the time, Lamb, who entered the school soon after Coleridge, has left us a vivid picture. Food was scanty and unappetising ; those who, like Coleridge, were far from home and had no means of obtaining anything extra often suffered actually from hunger, particularly on the long holidays when the boys were turned out all day to look after themselves. The discipline, under Boyer, was of the severest. He caned continually ; and the monitors exercised their right freely, also, on the younger boys. Yet there were compensations. Boyer was a sound and intelligent classical scholar, and a man of wide reading who gave his pupils a real appreciation of good literature, insisting on parallel study of the English masters along with the classics. He also encouraged the boys in their own writing—only checking with decision and vigour any tendency towards what he deemed fantastic or sentimental. Coleridge, though he did not like him, acknowledged many years after, the debt he owed him for his guidance in matters of literary taste. Further, Coleridge soon won in the school a group of friends and admirers, one, at least, of whom was to remain faithful to him through life. It is this friend, Charles Lamb, who has drawn him for us as he appeared to his school-fellows—already, while a youth, " logician, metaphysician, bard," forcing the " casual passer " to " stand still, entranced with admiration (while he weighed the disproportion between the speech and the garb of the young Mirandula)," to listen to the boy pouring out philosophy or poetry, " while the walls of the old Grey Friars re-echoed with the accents of the *inspired charity-boy*." His marvellous gift of eloquence had already become evident. As a poet his future genius was not so unmistakably foreshadowed. His early poems were frequently written as school exercises for Dr. Boyer, and they show no remarkable poetic power. They are strongly influenced by earlier eighteenth-century writers, and are marred by what he himself described as " a profusion of double epithets and a general turgidness." Coleridge did not find himself in poetry before he lost himself in metaphysics— which happened, he tells us, before he reached his fifteenth year.

Two causes combined to win him back from the mazes of speculation into which he plunged. First, he fell in love at the age of sixteen, with Mary Evans, the sister of a schoolfellow, who, in return for kindness shown him at school, invited Coleridge to his home ; and, secondly, he was recalled to allegiance to poetry by receiving from a former schoolfellow, as a gift, a copy of the sonnets of a now long-forgotten poet, William Lisle Bowles. Inferior as these poems were, and destined to oblivion, for a time they exercised great influence over Coleridge. For in Bowles he discovered a poet who spoke with the voice of his own time, who described simply what he saw, and who gave some expression, at any rate, to the rising flood of emotionalism which was sweeping over Europe, to find outlet, just at this time, in its most vehement form, in the French Revolution. Coleridge hailed the "Destruction of the Bastille" in an ode which, set as a school exercise, is significant at least as herald of that flame of revolutionary ardour which blazed up in him so brightly during the next few years.

Meanwhile the "young Mirandula" went through various mental vicissitudes. Curiously enough, he was, he says, entirely without ambition ; and while he was promoted in the school to become a "Grecian"—one of the group of scholars who pass on to the University —he decided himself that he would like to become apprentice to a cobbler with whom he had made friends. He had, however, failed to take sufficiently into calculation Dr. Boyer, who drove the cobbler from the school with characteristic vigour and decision. The doctor's aid was next called in to "reconvert his pupil" from atheism "by means of a sound flogging" —afterwards described by Coleridge as "the only just one" he ever had from him.

A rage for medicine, which took possession of him when his brother, Luke, came up to study at the London Hospital, passed also, giving way again to "a rage for metaphysics."

Finally, after some months of rheumatic fever and other illness, brought on by carelessness in staying in wet clothes after swimming the New River, Coleridge left Christ's Hospital, in September 1789, to enter Jesus College, Cambridge, early in the following year, with a leaving exhibition given on the tacit understanding that the holder should read for the Church.

Before he entered college he had lost his elder brother, Luke, and his only sister, whom he had loved devotedly. It was the memory of this loss that especially roused his sympathies with Charles Lamb, who consecrated his life to the care of his afflicted sister, Mary. It is to this that he refers in a poem " To a Friend " (Charles Lamb), sent to him, "with an unfinished poem." Though it was not written till some four years later, it may fittingly find place here :

TO A FRIEND

Thus far my scanty brain hath built the rhyme
Elaborate and swelling : yet the heart
Not owns it. From thy spirit-breathing powers
I ask not now, my friend ! the aiding verse,
Tedious to thee, and from thy anxious thought
Of dissonant mood. In fancy (well I know)
From business wandering far and local cares,
Thou creepest round a dear-loved Sister's bed
With noiseless step, and watchest the faint look,
Soothing each pang with fond solicitude,
And tenderest tones medicinal of love.
I too a Sister had, an only Sister—
She loved me dearly, and I doted on her !
To her I pour'd forth all my puny sorrows,

B

COLERIDGE & HIS POETRY

(As sick Patient in his Nurse's arms)
And of the heart those hidden maladies
That even from Friendship's eye will shrink ashamed
O ! I have woke at midnight, and have wept,
Because she was not !—Cheerily, dear Charles !
Thou thy best friend shalt cherish many a year :
Such warm presagings feel I of high Hope.
For not uninterested the dear Maid
I've view'd—her soul affectionate yet wise,
Her polish'd wit as mild as lambent glories
That play around a sainted infant's head.
He knows (the Spirit that in secret sees,
Of whose omniscient and all-spreading Love
Aught to *implore* were impotence of mind)
That my mute thoughts are sad before His throne,
Prepared, when He His healing ray vouchsafes,
To pour forth thanksgiving with lifted heart,
And praise Him Gracious with a Brother's Joy !

II

For some time after Coleridge took up his residence in Cambridge, his application to regular academic studies sustained that promise of future brilliant achievement in classics with which he had left Christ's Hospital. He gained a prize for a Greek Sapphic ode, obtained a sizarship, and entered for a scholarship. But, from various causes, this industry did not last. We have seen him as a schoolboy, distinguishing himself in his set tasks, yet taking refuge continually in himself and in philosophical speculations, to cure him of which his master had no better remedy than a flogging ; we have seen

him fired with the dream of Liberty, that
possessed young England on the outbreak of the
Revolution ; we have seen him won again to
the love of poetry by the voice of a contemporary
who spoke the language of his time. Against
these influences a scholarship that had only
touched his intellect and for which in itself he
was always unambitious, while its method had
rather hindered than given scope to his origi-
nality, soon competed in vain.

The first of the disturbing influences was the
French Revolution. Charles le Grice, a Blue-
coat boy, who followed him to Cambridge,
describes the meetings in his room of " conver-
sation-loving friends, . . . when Æschylus
and Plato and Thucydides were pushed aside,
with a pile of lexicons, &c., to discuss the
pamphlets of the day. Ever and anon, a
pamphlet issued from the pen of Burke. There
was no need of having the book before us.
Coleridge had read it in the morning, and in
the evening he would repeat whole pages
verbatim."

Coleridge had greeted the Fall of the Bastille,
in the poem already referred to, as herald of the
time when

> Liberty, the soul of Life, shall reign,
> Shall throb in every pulse, shall flow thro' every vein !

As the Revolution went from horror to horror,
first alarming then alienating its early sup-
porters in England, Coleridge for some time
remained ardent in its support. For from the

beginning it was the principles which underlay the Revolution that fired his enthusiasm ; not so much sympathy with oppressed men as fervour for the cause of Freedom (written with a capital) ; for a time abstract theories of " human perfectibility " possessed him ; Utopian dreams filled his thoughts. So at Cambridge he declaimed and theorised ; made himself prominent as upholder of all whom he deemed friends of liberty or sufferers from tyranny ; and became the centre of an admiring, sympathising group, who enjoyed his eloquence and were carried away by the warmth and brilliance of his monologues.

While Southey at Oxford was openly defying college conventions, Coleridge at Cambridge was indifferently neglecting them. Gillman tells an anecdote of the way he received a reproof from the master of Jesus College for " his appearance not being in collegiate trim." His fellow-students had amused themselves at lectures by cutting off pieces of his gown, till its length was considerably diminished. Clad in the remains, he was met by the master :

" Mr. Coleridge ! Mr. Coleridge ! when will you get rid of that shameful gown ? "

Coleridge promptly replied, with ready repartee : " Why, sir, I think I've got rid of the greatest part of it already."

Early taking an independent standpoint with regard to college régime, and in revolt against the principles of University government, Coleridge, after spending the long vacation of 1793 at Ottery, suddenly took one of the most erratic and irresponsible steps in what was henceforth to be an all too irresponsible life. Shortly after his return to Cambridge in the autumn he fled from the University, and enlisted in the 15th or King's Regiment of Light Dragoons, under the name of Silas Tomkyn Comberbacke. Why he did this has never been satisfactorily explained. It has been put down to worry over debts accidentally incurred ; and to disappointment over the rejection of his love by Mary Evans. Whatever the cause, for two months he remained a private in the regiment, and his friends knew nothing of his whereabouts. The idea of Coleridge, the ardent revolutionary, hater of war, and entertainer, as he tells us, of " a violent antipathy to soldiers and horses," serving as private in the British army is not a little humorous. To his fellow-soldiers he presented a humorous figure also. He could neither ride nor look after his horse, and tradition says that he used to write verses and love-letters for the soldiers in return for their grooming it. Eventually a friend who met him by chance in the streets of Reading revealed his whereabouts, and after some correspondence, his discharge, for which he now was as eager as his friends, was obtained.

He returned to Cambridge, where he was received with a mild reproof and slight punishment. But before the term ended he again left the town, and—though he returned once more— at the close of 1794, without a degree, because of his refusal to assent to the theological tests then imposed, he left Cambridge, and his college career came to an end.

By this time, however, his head was full of a new project, which, if carried out, would make a degree quite superfluous. This was none other than the wildly Utopian scheme of the Pantisocracy, planned with Southey, with whom a rapid friendship had sprung up, on a visit which Coleridge paid to Oxford in the summer of his last year at college. These young enthusiasts believed that Europe as a whole had mistaken the meaning of the French Revolution. England, in declaring war against France, was guilty of treason to the cause of freedom. Escaping from the trammels of a degenerate civilisation, far from the sway of tyrants, they, Coleridge and Southey, would found a new State, would show to the world that the principles which underlay the Revolution were right, and that to follow them out logically would be to find happiness. A new name had to be coined to fit the scheme—one that implied no division of classes, for there was to be none. " Pantisocracy " was chosen. In America, on the banks of the Susquehanna, the dream was to be realised. The number of colonists was at first limited to twenty-four—twelve men and twelve women. It was judged that two or three hours' work a day on the part of the men would be sufficient to provide for all material needs, the products of industry to be shared in common. Unfortunately for the scheme, neither of the projectors had the wherewithal necessary to embark on it. Another difficulty, the finding of wives for the colonists, was, as we shall see, more easily overcome. A third, perhaps as practical as any, was suggested to Coleridge by some friends at Cambridge to whom he talked for six hours on the subject, and who concluded by agreeing that pantisocracy was " impregnable, supposing the assigned quantum of virtue and genius in the first individuals."

Money being the most pressing necessity, Coleridge and Southey set to work to see how they could get together what was required. After an unsuccessful attempt at a joint drama, " The Fall of Robespierre," each undertook a set of lectures in Bristol, whither Coleridge had gone to join Southey. It is on record that Coleridge, already wandering and irregular, succeeded in earning only a quarter of what his painstaking friend earned, and was therefore largely kept by him.

Here Coleridge met his first publisher, Joseph Cottle, who offered him thirty guineas for a collection of his poems, which he accordingly set to work to prepare, and which appeared in 1796. Meanwhile, Southey's enthusiasm for the great scheme had begun to die down as he realised its impracticability, and finally, to Coleridge's intense temporary indignation, he withdrew altogether. But it had involved Coleridge in at least one momentous step. The necessity of finding wives for the colonists has already been referred to. When Coleridge first went to Bristol, Southey was engaged to Edith Fricker, the daughter of a Bristol tradesman. Another of the participators in the scheme became engaged to her sister, and Coleridge, fresh from his disappointment with Mary Evans, began to pay addresses to Sarah, the eldest daughter.

On October 4, 1795, at St. Mary's Redcliffe, Bristol, they were married. That he was at the time genuinely in love is proved undoubtedly by contemporary evidence and by his own writings. The marriage was followed by an idyllic honeymoon in a little cottage at Clevedon. And here, under the inspiration of love and happiness, Coleridge produced, in the '' Æolian Harp,'' one of the first of his poems in which, standing on his own ground, he combined independent poetic achievement with some foreshadowing of the greatness to come.

But it was not Coleridge's lot thus to stay long '' and tranquil muse upon tranquillity.'' Whether he tired of the seclusion, or whether the '' bread-and-cheese question '' became too pressing, or whether, as he sang in a farewell poem, the thought that '' unnumbered brethren toiled and bled '' while he dreamt away '' the entrusted hours,'' impelled him to return, by the end of the year he was again in Bristol. And now, Pantisocracy forgotten, he entertained various projects for supporting a home. For a few months he edited a paper called '' The Watchman,'' but it came to an end for the all-sufficient reason that it did not pay expenses.

24

Then he took into his home as pupil the son of a Quaker acquaintance, Charles Lloyd, who brought with him £80 a year as a help towards the housekeeping, just when Coleridge's eldest son, David Hartley, was born.

At last, after some months of freely voiced despair as to future prospects—despair as ominous as the fact noted in a letter to a friend that he was taking laudanum to relieve neuralgic pains—Coleridge decided to give up the attempt to lead a public life, and to take up his abode in a little cottage in the Quantock village of Nether Stowey, in order to be near a friend whom he had met at Bristol, Thomas Poole, whose admiration of his genius and staunch friendship never failed during the trying years that followed.

It was to him that Coleridge, on the eve of his sublimest achievements in poetry, wrote : " My poetic vanity and my political furor have been exhaled, and I would rather be an expert self-maintaining gardener than a Milton, if I could not unite both." So little did he know himself.

The beginning of 1797 saw the would-be gardener settled with his wife and child and with Lloyd in the cottage at Nether Stowey. " I mean," he wrote, " to work *very hard*— as Cook, Butler, Scullion, Shoe-cleaner, occasional Nurse, Gardener, Hind, Pig-protector, Chaplain, Secretary, Poet, Reviewer, and *omnium-botherum* Sinhillg-scavenger. In other words, I shall keep no servant, and shall cultivate my land-acre and my wiseacres as well as I can."

III

In going to Nether Stowey Coleridge took what proved to be the most momentous decision of his poetic life. It opened up for him nearly two years of such happiness as he had not hitherto known ; it brought him within reach of the influences of nature at a time when his sensibilities were at their keenest ; and it gave to him friends, in the sunshine of whose affection and understanding his genius blossomed and bore fruit of such a kind as there had before been little promise of, and such as, after the brief period was over, was never again to be put forth. Coleridge was in one way peculiarly responsive to external influences. To his wife he once wrote, " I am deeply convinced that if I were to remain a few years among objects for whom I had no affection I should wholly lose the powers of intellect. Love is the vital air of my genius." In the next two years he was to win the friendship and intellectual sympathy of one of the few men he ever met whom he felt to be the possessor of greater genius, and in freedom of intercourse with whom he reached the supreme height of his poetic achievement.

But before entering into a further account of this happy period, we must return for a moment to close another chapter in Coleridge's history, and trace to its conclusion the story of his connection with the French Revolution.

Just as he left Bristol, at the close of 1796, Coleridge wrote an " Ode on the Departing

Year." It is filled with passionate declamation against " the brood of Hell," the kings who had combined against France ; with indignation with his country, which had " join'd the wild yelling of Famine and Blood." But the conclusion is significant. Coleridge having performed his task of prophetic denunciation, washes his hands of it and, " unpartaking of the evil thing,"

Now I recentre my immortal mind
In the deep sabbath of meek self-content ;
Cleansed from the vaporous passions that bedim
God's Image, sister of the Seraphim.

When Coleridge could contemplate drawing aloof in this way his enthusiasm was evidently cooling ; yet it was not till rather more than a year later that he made formal recantation. Then France, in attacking Switzerland, destroyed all possibility of belief any longer that she was the champion of freedom. Disillusionment was complete, and in the following poem, entitled " France : An Ode," or " Recantation," Coleridge gave it completest expression :

FRANCE : AN ODE

I

Ye Clouds ! that far above me float and pause,
  Whose pathless march no mortal may controul !
  Ye Ocean-Waves ! that, wheresoe'er ye roll,
Yield homage only to eternal laws !
Ye Woods ! that listen to the night-birds' singing,
  Midway the smooth and perilous slope reclined,

27

Save when your own imperious branches swinging,
   Have made a solemn music of the wind !
Where, like a man beloved of God,
Through glooms, which never woodman trod,
    How oft, pursuing fancies holy,
My moonlight way o'er flowering weeds I wound,
    Inspired, beyond the guess of folly,
By each rude shape and wild unconquerable sound !
O ye loud Waves ! and O ye Forests high !
   And O ye Clouds that far above me soared !
Thou rising Sun ! thou blue rejoicing Sky !
   Yea, every thing that is and will be free !
   Bear witness for me, wheresoe'er ye be,
   With what deep worship I have still adored
    The spirit of divinest Liberty.

II

When France in wrath her giant-limbs upreared,
   And with that oath, which smote air, earth, and
    sea,
   Stamped her strong foot and said she would be free,
Bear witness for me, how I hoped and feared !
With what a joy my lofty gratulation
   Unawed I sang, amid a slavish band :
And when to whelm the disenchanted nation,
   Like fiends embattled by a wizard's wand,
    The Monarchs marched in evil day,
     And Britain join'd the dire array ;
   Though dear her shores and circling ocean,
Though many friendships, many youthful loves
   Had swoln the patriot emotion
And flung a magic light o'er all her hills and groves ;
Yet still my voice, unaltered, sang defeat
   To all that braved the tyrant-quelling lance,
And shame too long delay'd and vain retreat !

For ne'er, O Liberty ! with partial aim
I dimmed thy light or damped thy holy flame ;
  But blessed the pæans of delivered France,
And hung my head and wept at Britain's name.

III

" And what," I said, " though Blasphemy's loud
    scream
  With that sweet music of deliverance strove !
  Though all the fierce and drunken passions wove
A dance more wild than e'er was maniac's dream !
  Ye storms, that round the dawning east assembled,
The Sun was rising, though ye hid his light ! "
    And when, to soothe my soul, that hoped and
        trembled,
The dissonance ceased, and all seemed calm and bright ;
  When France her front deep-scarr'd and gory
  Concealed with clustering wreaths of glory ;
    When, insupportably advancing,
  Her arm made mockery of the warrior's ramp ;
    While timid looks of fury glancing,
  Domestic treason, crushed beneath her fatal stamp
Writhed like a wounded dragon in his gore ;
  Then I reproached my fears that would not flee ;
" And soon," I said, " shall Wisdom teach her lore
In the low huts of them that toil and groan !
And, conquering by her happiness alone,
  Shall France compel the nations to be free,
Till Love and Joy look round, and call the Earth their
    own."

IV

Forgive me, Freedom ! O forgive those dreams !
  I hear thy voice, I hear thy loud lament,
  From bleak Helvetia's icy caverns sent—
I hear thy groans upon her blood-stained streams !

Heroes, that for your peaceful country perished,
And ye that, fleeing, spot your mountain-snows
    With bleeding wounds ; forgive me, that I
        cherished
One thought that ever blessed your cruel foes !
    To scatter rage and traitorous guilt
    Where Peace her jealous home had built ;
        A patriot-race to disinherit
Of all that made their stormy wilds so dear ;
        And with inexpiable spirit
To taint the bloodless freedom of the mountaineer—
O France, that mockest Heaven, adulterous, blind,
    And patriot only in pernicious toils !
Are these thy boasts, Champion of human kind ?
    To mix with Kings in the low lust of sway,
Yell in the hunt, and share the murderous prey ;
To insult the shrine of Liberty with spoils
    From freemen torn ; to tempt and to betray ?

V

    The Sensual and the Dark rebel in vain,
    Slaves by their own compulsion ! In mad game
    They burst their manacles and wear the name
        Of Freedom, graven on a heavier chain !
O Liberty ! with profitless endeavour
Have I pursued thee, many a weary hour ;
    But thou nor swell'st the victor's strain, nor ever
Didst breathe thy soul in forms of human power.
    Alike from all, howe'er they praise thee,
        (Nor prayer, nor boastful name delays thee]
        Alike from Priestcraft's harpy minions,
    And factious Blasphemy's obscener slaves,
        Thou speedest on thy subtle pinions,
The guide of homeless winds, and playmate of the
        waves !

COLERIDGE & HIS POETRY

And there I felt thee !—on that sea-cliff's verge,
  Whose pines, scarce travelled by the breeze above
Had made one murmur with the distant surge !
Yes, while I stood and gazed, my temples bare,
And shot my being through earth, sea and air,
  Possessing all things with intensest love,
    O Liberty ! my spirit felt thee there.

This magnificent poem Shelley pronounced
"the finest ode in the English language."
Thought and feeling combine in "solemn
music," charged with genuine passion. It
was the greatest as (except for the blank verse
"Fears in Solitude") it was the last of the
poems produced under the influence of revolutionary enthusiasm. Thenceforth Coleridge,
former Pantisocrat, now linked to his country
by tender, recently formed ties of home affection, turned into a warm patriot, and eventually
into a strong Conservative.

The story of his connection with the Revolution is interesting for the light it throws on his
character. At the first outburst his feelings
caught fire, and he threw himself with un-
restrained ardour into the fight on the side of
the people. But, as he said truly of himself
later, "I feel strongly and I think strongly, but
I seldom feel without thinking or think without feeling." And he was soon at work formu-
lating intellectual theories which justified and
reinforced the ardour he exhibited. As always,
he showed keen power of analysis and depth of
insight into principles. That the facts of the
Revolution failed to come up to the level

required by the abstract theories was "so much the worse for the facts." The feelings roused, therefore, by the actual events at the beginning, died down. But the intellectual structure of abstract principles remained. At the beginning of the Revolution Coleridge had hailed the advent of " divine liberty " as a natural development of universal history. Over this bridge he passed, in the ode just quoted, with very little struggle considering the violence of his early feelings, from the camp of Revolution to the camp of Conservatism, believing that the advent of " divine liberty " would yet be, in the due course of natural development, when men, no longer " sensual and dark," should be ready to partake of it.

The cottage into which Coleridge moved at Nether Stowey was small and unpretentious, but it had two great attractions. It possessed over an acre of garden, and it was quite close to the house of Thomas Poole. Poole was a man of remarkable character. " A stout, plain-looking farmer," as De Quincey describes him, " leading a bachelor life in a rustic, old-fashioned house," and largely self-educated, he was distinguished for wide culture, great discrimination, and generous sympathies. He was the friend of many famous men and " the guide and counsellor " to " his humble fellow-countrymen . . . for many miles round."

Before Coleridge came to settle near him Poole had already given him pecuniary assistance in a very delicate way. Now mutual

32

benefit was derived from close and continual intercourse, while Nether Stowey for a while became a centre of culture and literary output that gave direction to the poetry of the nineteenth century.

The first important arrivals in the neighbourhood after Coleridge settled there were William and Dorothy Wordsworth. Wordsworth had met Coleridge in Bristol, and soon afterwards Coleridge had paid them a visit at Racedown, on the border of Dorset, where they were then living. A friendship rapidly sprang up between them. In June 1797 the Wordsworths visited Coleridge at Nether Stowey, and finding Alfoxden, a house in the neighbourhood, was to let, they took it, attracted, as Dorothy Wordsworth tells us, by the prospect of Coleridge's society. He had won her admiration at their first meeting.

" At first," she says, " I thought him very plain, that is for about three minutes : he is pale, thin, has a wide mouth, thick lips, and not very good teeth, longish, loose-growing, half-curling, rough black hair. But, if you hear him speak for five minutes you think no more of them. His eye is large and full, and not very dark, but grey—such an eye as would receive from a heavy soul the dullest expression ; but it speaks every emotion of his animated mind ; it has more of ' the poet's eye in a fine frenzy rolling ' than I ever witnessed. He has fine dark eyebrows and an overhanging forehead."

While the Wordsworths were with Coleridge, Lamb came to pay a long-promised visit. Cole-

ridge, by an unfortunate accident, was unable
to walk during the whole of his stay.   One day,
while the Wordsworths were taking their friend
on a favourite walk in the neighbourhood,
Coleridge, sitting alone in his garden, wrote for
him the following poem :

THIS LIME-TREE BOWER MY PRISON
ADDRESSED TO CHARLES LAMB

Well, they are gone, and here must I remain,
This lime-tree bower my prison !   I have lost
Beauties and feelings, such as would have been
Most sweet to my remembrance even when age
Had dimmed mine eyes to blindness !   They, mean-
    while,
Friends, whom I never more may meet again,
On springy heath, along the hill-top edge,
Wander in gladness, and wind down, perchance,
To that still roaring dell, of which I told ;
The roaring dell, o'erwooded, narrow, deep,
And only speckled by the midday sun ;
Where its slim trunk the ash from rock to rock
Flings arching like a bridge ; —that branchless ash,
Unsunned and damp, whose few poor yellow leaves
Ne'er tremble in the gale, yet tremble still,
Fanned by the water-fall ! and there my friends
Behold the dark green file of long lank weeds,
That all at once (a most fantastic sight !)
Still nod and drip beneath the dripping edge
Of the blue clay-stone.

                Now, my friends emerge
Beneath the wide wide Heaven—and view again
The many-steepled tract magnificent

34

Of hilly fields and meadows, and the sea,
With some fair bark, perhaps, whose sails light up
The slip of smooth clear blue betwixt two Isles
Of purple shadow ! Yes ! they wander on
In gladness all ; but thou, methinks, most glad,
My gentle-hearted Charles ! for thou hast pined
And hungered after Nature, many a year,
In the great City pent, winning thy way
With sad yet patient soul, through evil and pain
And strange calamity ! Ah ! slowly sink
Behind the western ridge, thou glorious Sun !
Shine in the slant beams of the sinking orb,
Ye purple heath-flowers ! richlier burn, ye clouds !
Live in the yellow light, ye distant groves !
And kindle, thou blue Ocean ! So my Friend
Struck with deep joy may stand, as I have stood,
Silent with swimming sense ; yea, gazing round
On the wide landscape, gaze till all doth seem
Less gross than bodily ; and of such hues
As veil the Almighty Spirit, when yet he makes
Spirits perceive his presence.

                  A delight
Comes sudden on my heart, and I am glad
As I myself were there ! Nor in this bower,
This little lime-tree bower, have I not marked
Much that has soothed me. Pale beneath the blaze
Hung the transparent foliage ; and I watched
Some broad and sunny leaf, and loved to see
The shadow of the leaf and stem above,
Dappling its sunshine ! And that walnut-tree
Was richly tinged, and a deep radiance lay
Full on the ancient ivy, which usurps
Those fronting elms, and now, with blackest mass
Makes their dark branches gleam a lighter hue
Through the late twilight : and though now the bat

35

Wheels silent by, and not a swallow twitters,
Yet still the solitary humble-bee
Sings in the bean-flower !   Henceforth I shall know
That Nature ne'er deserts the wise and pure ;
No plot so narrow, be but Nature there,
No waste so vacant, but may well employ
Each faculty of sense, and keep the heart
Awake to Love and Beauty ! and sometimes
'Tis well to be bereft of promised good,
That we may lift the soul, and contemplate
With lively joy the joys we cannot share.
My gentle-hearted Charles ! when the last rook
Beat its straight path along the dusky air
Homewards, I blest it ! deeming, its black wing
(Now a dim speck, now vanishing in light)
Had cross'd the mighty orb's dilated glory,
While thou stood'st gazing ; or when all was still,
Flew creeking o'er thy head, and had a charm
For thee, my gentle-hearted Charles, to whom
No sound is dissonant which tells of Life.

This is a most charming example of the poetry of natural description combined with patriotic feeling and human interest, of which Coleridge was at once originator and master.

The story of Coleridge's friendship with Lamb is one of the pleasantest of a life that, with all its varied fortunes, was rich in friendships. He understood Lamb's reserved, sensitive nature, and his affection and sympathy were Lamb's greatest solace through years of trouble. In return Lamb gave to Coleridge unstinted but discriminating admiration, and, except for one brief period of misunderstanding, unswerving loyalty to the day of his death.

COLERIDGE & HIS POETRY

Another poem, written in the same year, is "Kubla Khan." Here Coleridge for the first time steps on to the borders of magic ground. Twice more he found the way there, and then the door was shut and the key turned for ever.

Of the origin of "Kubla Khan" he gives the following account: "In the summer of 1797 the author, then in ill-health, had retired to a lonely farmhouse between Porlock and Linton. . . . In consequence of a slight indisposition, an anodyne had been prescribed, from the effects of which he fell asleep in his chair at the moment that he was reading the following sentence, or words of the same substance, in Purchas's 'Pilgrimage': 'Here the Kubla Khan commanded a palace to be built, and a stately garden thereunto. And thus ten miles of fertile ground were enclosed by a wall.' The author continued for about three hours in a profound sleep, at least of the external senses, during which time he has the most vivid confidence that he could not have composed less than from two to three hundred lines; if that indeed can be called composition in which all the images rose up before him as things, with a parallel production of the corresponding expressions, without any sensation or consciousness of effort. On awaking he appeared to himself to have a distinct recollection of the whole, and, taking his pen, ink, and paper, instantly and eagerly wrote down the lines that are here preserved."

COLERIDGE & HIS POETRY

KUBLA KHAN

In Xanadu did Kubla Khan
A stately pleasure-dome decree :
Where Alph, the sacred river, ran
Through caverns measureless to man
    Down to a sunless sea.
So twice five miles of fertile ground
With walls and towers were girdled round :
And here were gardens bright with sinuous rills,
Where blossomed many an incense-bearing tree ;
And here were forests ancient as the hills,
Enfolding sunny spots of greenery.

But oh ! that deep romantic chasm which slanted
Down the green hill athwart a cedarn cover !
A savage place ! as holy and enchanted
As e'er beneath a waning moon was haunted
By woman wailing for her demon-lover !
And from this chasm, with ceaseless turmoil seething,
As if this earth in fast thick pants were breathing,
A mighty fountain momently was forced :
Amid whose swift half-intermitted burst
Huge fragments vaulted like rebounding hail,
Or chaffy grain beneath the thresher's flail :
And 'mid these dancing rocks at once and ever
It flung up momently the sacred river.
Five miles meandering with a mazy motion
Through wood and dale the sacred river ran,
Then reached the caverns measureless to man,
And sank in tumult to a lifeless ocean :
And 'mid this tumult Kubla heard from far
Ancestral voices prophesying war !

    The shadow of the dome of pleasure
    Floated midway on the waves ;

COLERIDGE & HIS POETRY

Where was heard the mingled measure
From the fountain and the caves.
It was a miracle of rare device,
A sunny pleasure-dome with caves of ice !

A damsel with a dulcimer
In a vision once I saw :
It was an Abyssinian maid,
And on her dulcimer she played,
Singing of Mount Abora.
Could I revive within me
Her symphony and song,
To such a deep delight 'twould win me,
That with music loud and long,
I would build that dome in air,
That sunny dome ! those caves of ice !
And all who heard should see them there,
And all should cry, Beware ! Beware !
His flashing eyes, his floating hair !
Weave a circle round him thrice,
And close your eyes with holy dread,
For he on honey-dew hath fed,
And drunk the milk of Paradise.

At this point an inopportune caller interrupted
the poet, and when '' above an hour '' later he
returned to the poem, '' with the exception of
some eight or ten scattered lines and images,
all the rest had passed away like the images on
the surface of a stream into which a stone had
been cast, but, alas ! without the after restora-
tion of the latter.''

The poem is therefore only a fragment. As
might be expected from the curious circumstances of its production, it does not contain

any " coherent body of thought." But for the interruption it might have been continued, but never completed. Yet what a glorious fragment it is ! A dazzling succession of gorgeous images caught at the moment of inspiration, and set to witching music—haunting, unforgettable.

It was on hearing Coleridge repeat this poem some years later that Lamb wrote : " He repeats it so enchantingly that it irradiates and brings heaven and Elysian bowers into my parlour when he sings or says it . . . his face when he repeats his verses hath its ancient glory ; an archangel a little damaged."

In yet another way the poem was significant. In its freedom of rhythm, its " revolutionary violence " of imagination, its utter abandonment to the inspiration of the moment, " Kubla Khan " marks the extreme revolt against the formal, restrained, and artificial diction of the poets of the early part of the eighteenth century. It heralds the complete emancipation of English poetry from their influence, to be effected largely by the productions of Coleridge and Wordsworth in the months that followed.

IV

The establishment of the Wordsworths at Alfoxden in July 1797 was the beginning of a period of closest intercourse. Dorothy Wordsworth's " Journal " records almost daily interchange of visits between Alfoxden and Nether Stowey. Long rambles over the tree-clad valleys and green hills of the Quantocks were undertaken together, Dorothy usually being of the company. "We were three people," says Coleridge, "but only one soul." The three were attracted to one another in mutual admiration. Dorothy's description of Coleridge we have already read. Wordsworth long after bore his testimony to the powers of "the most *wonderful* man" he ever knew.

> Upon smooth Quantock's airy ridge we roved
> Unchecked, or loitered 'mid her sylvan combs,

rejoicing in common love of poetry and of nature, in aims held in common, and in equal friendship. For each of the poets possessed something which the other had not. Coleridge's intellect was quick, versatile, and penetrating ; Wordsworth's was less versatile but more deeply meditative. Coleridge was idealistic, and ranged far in the realms of abstract thought ; Wordsworth, though he transformed them by the imagination, sought his inspiration among the things of everyday. How far they influenced each other directly and who gained most by the friendship are matters of discussion. But the recognition by each that their spheres were different, and that each was complementary to the other, gave rise to the most important production of the close of the century. This was none other than the epoch-making volume of poems known as the "Lyrical Ballads."

Of the origin of the book Coleridge, in the "Biographia Literaria," has given the following account. On their long rambles together the conversation between him and Wordsworth " frequently turned on the two cardinal points of poetry, the power of exciting the sympathy of the reader by a faithful adherence to the truth of nature, and the power of giving the interest of novelty by the modifying colours of the imagination. . . . The thought suggested itself (to which of us I do not recollect) that a series of poems might be composed of two sorts. In the one, the incidents and agents were to be, in part at least, supernatural ; and the excellence aimed at was to consist in the interesting of the affections by the dramatic truth of such emotions as would naturally accompany such situations, supposing them real. . . . For the second class subjects were to be chosen from ordinary life ; the characters and incidents were to be such as will be found in every village and its vicinity where there is a meditative and feeling mind to seek after them, or to notice them when they present themselves. In this idea originated the plan of the ' Lyrical Ballads,' in which it was agreed that my endeavours should be directed to persons and characters supernatural, or at least romantic ; yet so as to transfer from our inward nature a human interest and a semblance of truth sufficient to procure for these shadows of imagination that willing suspension of disbelief for the moment, which constitutes poetic faith. Mr. Wordsworth, on the other hand, was to propose to himself as his object, to give the charm of novelty to things of every day, and to excite a feeling analogous to the supernatural by awakening the mind's attention from the lethargy of custom, and directing it to the loveliness and the wonders of the world before us.''

In order to understand the significance of the aims which the two young poets thus set before themselves, it is necessary to pause for a moment and consider briefly the character of the poetry of the early and middle eighteenth century in England, and also of the tendencies that had been manifesting themselves towards the close. The Augustan Age of English literature—for such was the title claimed for themselves by the writers of the Age of Anne—was essentially an artificial age. Its literature was a polished, city literature, and it was markedly lacking in certain allied qualities. It had little genuine feeling, little true appreciation of nature, little sense of '' wonder and mystery,'' and no interest in the romantic past. Its highest ideal of poetry was unimpassioned reasoning in verse, and epigrammatic wit. But about the middle of the century a reaction began. The wave of emotionalism which swept over Europe, and of which the French Revolution, as we have noticed, was but one outcome, showed its influence in literature in a revived interest in two chief directions. Men began again to turn to the '' romantic '' past of the Middle Ages as a source of inspiration ; they began also to go direct to nature and to describe what they saw

43

there simply and accurately. Thus the two streams of romanticism and naturalism came into English poetry. But to prevent its running to wild excesses, romance needed the touch of reality ; to prevent its becoming unimaginative and material, naturalism needed the touch of romance. On the Quantock Hills in the years 1797–1798 the two streams flowed into one. In the " Lyrical Ballads " Coleridge and Wordsworth, between them, solved the problem of how to make the romantic natural and the natural romantic.

Coleridge's great contribution to the " Lyrical Ballads " was " The Ancient Mariner," " his one perfect and complete achievement." The way in which this marvellous poem came to be written was commonplace enough. On the afternoon of November 13, 1797, Coleridge, Wordsworth, and his sister set off together from Alfoxden on a walking expedition, " with a view," Wordsworth tells us, " to visit Linton and the Valley of Stones near to it ; and as our united funds were very small, we agreed to defray the expense of the tour by writing a poem to be sent to the ' New Monthly Magazine.' Accordingly we set off, and proceeded along the Quantock Hills towards Watchet ; and in the course of this walk was planned the poem of the ' Ancient Mariner,' founded on a dream, as Mr. Coleridge said, of his friend Mr. Cruikshank "
—a dream of a skeleton ship manned by skeleton sailors. With this dream as starting-point, other hints and suggestions were taken from

44

various sources. Wordsworth, who had been reading in Shelvocke's "Voyages" about the albatrosses of the South Seas, suggested that the mariner should be represented "as having killed one of these birds on entering the South Sea, and that the tutelary spirits of these regions take upon them to avenge the crime." He also contributed a few lines, but soon the manners of the two "proved so widely different" that he withdrew, and Coleridge completed the work himself. With consummate skill he welded the story into an artistic whole. For vividness of imagery and descriptive power the poem is unsurpassed. We move in a world of "unearthly weirdness," whose mystery and charm is unbroken by any inconsistency. We see the invisible and almost touch the intangible in this realm, where the things that are too seldom "dreamt of in our philosophy" loom within our ken. Absolutely simple in both metre and language, the poem is indeed, as Coleridge himself pronounced it, "inimitable." The story may well speak for itself.

THE RIME OF THE ANCIENT MARINER
PART I

It is an ancient Mariner,
And he stoppeth one of three.
"By thy long grey beard and glittering eye,
Now wherefore stopp'st thou me?

The Bridegroom's doors are opened wide,
And I am next of kin;

An ancient Mariner meeteth three Gallants bidden to a wedding-feast, and detaineth one.

45

The guests are met, the feast is set :
May'st hear the merry din.''

He holds him with his skinny hand,
" There was a ship,'' quoth he.
" Hold off ! unhand me, grey-beard loon ! ''
Eftsoons his hand dropt he.

The Wedding-Guest is spellbound by the eye of the old seafaring man, and constrained to hear his tale.

He holds him with his glittering eye—
The Wedding-Guest stood still,
And listens like a three years' child :
The Mariner hath his will.

The Wedding-Guest sat on a stone :
He cannot choose but hear ;
And thus spake on that ancient man,
The bright-eyed Mariner.

" The ship was cheered, the harbour cleared,
Merrily did we drop
Below the kirk, below the hill,
Below the lighthouse top.

The Mariner tells how the ship sailed southward with a good wind and fair weather, till it reached the Line.

" The sun came up upon the left,
Out of the sea came he !
And he shone bright, and on the right
Went down into the sea.

" Higher and higher every day,
Till over the mast at noon—''
The Wedding-Guest here beat his breast,
For he heard the loud bassoon.

The Wedding-Guest heareth the bridal music; but the Mariner continueth his tale.

The bride had paced into the hall,
Red as a rose is she ;
Nodding their heads before her goes
The merry minstrelsy.

46

COLERIDGE & HIS POETRY

The Wedding-Guest he beat his breast,
Yet he cannot choose but hear ;
And thus spake on that ancient man, ,
The bright-eyed Mariner.

" And now the Storm-blast came, and he
Was tyrannous and strong :
He struck with his o'ertaking wings,
And chased us south along.

The ship
driven by a
storm toward
the South
Pole.

" With sloping masts and dipping prow,
As who pursued with yell and blow
Still treads the shadow of his foe,
And forward bends his head,
The ship drove fast, loud roared the blast,
And southward aye we fled.

" And now there came both mist and snow,
And it grew wondrous cold :
And ice, mast-high, came floating by,
As green as emerald.

" And through the drifts the snowy clifts
Did send a dismal sheen :
Nor shapes of men nor beasts we ken—
The ice was all between.

The land of
ice, and of
fearful
sounds where
no living
thing was to
be seen.

" The ice was here, the ice was there,
The ice was all around :
It cracked and growled, and roared and
     howled,
Like noises in a swound !

" At length did cross an Albatross,
Thorough the fog it came ;
As if it had been a Christian soul,
We hailed it in God's name.

Till a great
sea-bird,
called the
Albatross,
came
through the
snow-fog,
and was re-
ceived with
great joy and
hospitality.

47

" It ate the food it ne'er had eat,
And round and round it flew.
The ice did split with a thunder-fit ;
The helmsman steered us through !

And lo ! the Albatross proveth a bird of good omen, and followeth the ship as it returned northward through fog and floating ice.

" And a good south wind sprung up behind ;
The Albatross did follow,
And every day, for food or play,
Came to the mariner's hollo !

" In mist or cloud, on mast or shroud,
It perched for vespers nine ;
Whiles all the night, through fog-smoke
   white,
Glimmered the white moon-shine."

The ancient Mariner inhospitably killeth the pious bird of good omen.

" God save thee, ancient Mariner !
From the fiends, that plague thee thus ! —
Why look'st thou so ? "—With my cross-bow
I shot the Albatross.

PART II

The Sun now rose upon the right :
Out of the sea came he,
Still hid in mist, and on the left
Went down into the sea.

And the good south wind still blew behind,
But no sweet bird did follow,
Nor any day for food or play
Came to the mariner's hollo !

His shipmates cry out against the ancient Mariner, for killing the bird of good luck.

And I had done a hellish thing,
And it would work 'em woe :
For all averred, I had killed the bird
That made the breeze to blow.
Ah wretch ! said they, the bird to slay,
That made the breeze to blow !

COLERIDGE & HIS POETRY

Nor dim nor red, like God's own head,
The glorious Sun uprist :
Then all averred, I had killed the bird
That brought the fog and mist.
'Twas right, said they, such birds to slay,
That bring the fog and mist.

But when the fog cleared off, they justify the same, and thus make themselves accomplices in the crime.

The fair breeze blew, the white foam flew,
The furrow followed free ;
We were the first that ever burst
Into that silent sea.

The fair breeze continues; the ship enters the Pacific Ocean, and sails northward, even till it reaches the Line.

Down dropt the breeze, the sails dropt down,
'Twas sad as sad could be ;
And we did speak only to break
The silence of the sea !

The ship hath been suddenly becalmed.

All in a hot and copper sky,
The bloody Sun, at noon,
Right up above the mast did stand,
No bigger than the Moon.

Day after day, day after day,
We stuck, nor breath nor motion ;
As idle as a painted ship
Upon a painted ocean.

Water, water, every where,
And all the boards did shrink ;
Water, water, every where
Nor any drop to drink.

And the Albatross begins to be avenged.

The very deep did rot : O Christ !
That ever this should be !
Yea, slimy things did crawl with legs
Upon the slimy sea.

D

49

About, about, in reel and rout
The death-fires danced at night ;
The water, like a witch's oils,
Burnt green, and blue and white.

A Spirit had followed them ; one of the invisible inhabitants of this planet, neither departed souls nor angels; concerning whom the learned Jew, Josephus, and the Platonic Constantinopolitan Michael Psellus, may be consulted. They are very numerous, and there is no climate or element without one or more.

And some in dreams assured were
Of the Spirit that plagued us so,
Nine fathom deep he had followed us
From the land of mist and snow.

And every tongue, through utter
     drought,
Was withered at the root ;
We could not speak, no more
     than if
We had been choked with soot.

The ship-mates, in their sore distress, would fain throw the whole guilt on the ancient Mariner ; in sign whereof they hang the dead sea-bird round his neck.

Ah ! well-a-day ! what evil looks
Had I from old and young !
Instead of the cross, the Albatross
About my neck was hung.

PART III

There passed a weary time.   Each throat
Was parched, and glazed each eye.

The ancient Mariner beholdeth a sign in the element afar off.

A weary time ! a weary time !
How glazed each weary eye,
When looking westward, I beheld
A something in the sky.

At first it seemed a little speck,
And then it seemed a mist ;
It moved and moved, and took at last
A certain shape, I wist.

A speck, a mist, a shape, I wist !
And still it neared and neared :
As if it dodged a water-sprite,
It plunged and tacked and veered.

50

With throats unslaked, with black lips baked,
We could nor laugh nor wail ;
Through utter drought all dumb we stood !
I bit my arm, I sucked the blood,
And cried, A sail ! a sail !

At its nearer approach, it seemeth him to be a ship ; and at a dear ransom he freeth his speech from the bonds of thirst.

With throats unslaked, with black lips baked,
Agape they heard me call :
Gramercy ! they for joy did grin,
And all at once their breath drew in,
As they were drinking all.

A flash of joy ;

See ! see ! (I cried) she tacks no more !
Hither to work us weal ;
Without a breeze, without a tide,
She steadies with upright keel !

And horror follows. For can it be a ship that comes onward without wind or tide ?

The western wave was all a-flame.
The day was wellnigh done !
Almost upon the western wave
Rested the broad bright Sun ;
When that strange shape drove suddenly
Betwixt us and the Sun.

And straight the Sun was flecked with bars,
(Heaven's Mother send us grace !)
As if through a dungeon-grate he peered
With broad and burning face.

It seemeth him but the skeleton of a ship.

Alas ! (thought I, and my heart beat loud)
How fast she nears and nears !
Are those her sails that glance in the Sun,
Like restless gossameres ?

Are those her ribs through which the Sun
Did peer, as through a grate ?
And is that Woman all her crew ?

And its ribs are seen as bars on the face of the setting Sun. The Spectre-Woman and

51

her Death-
mate, and no
other on
board the
skeleton-
ship.
Like vessel,
like crew!

Is that a Death ? and are there two ?
Is Death that woman's mate ?

Her lips were red, her looks were free,
Her locks were yellow as gold :
Her skin was as white as leprosy,
The Nightmare Life-in-Death was she,
Who thicks man's blood with cold.

Death and
Life-in-
Death have
diced for the
ship's crew,
and she (the
latter)
winneth the
ancient
Mariner.

The naked hulk alongside came,
And the twain were casting dice ;
" The game is done !   I've won !   I've
    won ! "
Quoth she, and whistles thrice.

No twilight
within the
courts of the
Sun.

The Sun's rim dips ; the stars rush out :
At one stride comes the dark ;
With far-heard whisper, o'er the sea,
Off shot the spectre-bark.

At the rising
of the Moon,

We listened and looked sideways up !
Fear at my heart, as at a cup,
My life-blood seemed to sip !
The stars were dim, and thick the night,
The steersman's face by his lamp gleamed
    white ;
From the sails the dew did drip—
Till clomb above the eastern bar
The horned Moon, with one bright star
Within the nether tip.

One after
another,

One after one, by the star-dogged Moon,
Too quick for groan or sigh,
Each turned his face with a ghastly pang,
And cursed me with his eye.

His ship-
mates drop
down dead.

Four times fifty living men,
(And I heard nor sigh nor groan)

With heavy thump, a lifeless lump,
They dropped down one by one.

The souls did from their bodies fly,—
They fled to bliss or woe !
And every soul, it passed me by,
Like the whizz of my cross-bow !

But Life-in-Death begins her work on the ancient Mariner.

PART IV

" I fear thee, ancient Mariner !
I fear thy skinny hand !
And thou art long, and lank, and brown,
As is the ribbed sea-sand.

The Wedding-Guest feareth that a Spirit is talking to him ;

" I fear thee and thy glittering eye,
And thy skinny hand, so brown.''—
Fear not, fear not, thou Wedding-Guest !
This body dropt not down.

But the ancient Mariner assureth him of his bodily life, and proceedeth to relate his horrible penance.

Alone, alone, all, all alone,
Alone on a wide wide sea !
And never a saint took pity on
My soul in agony.

The many men, so beautiful !
And they all dead did lie :
And a thousand thousand slimy things
Lived on ; and so did I.

He despiseth the creatures of the calm.

I looked upon the rotting sea,
And drew my eyes away ;
I looked upon the rotting deck,
And there the dead men lay.

And envieth that they should live, and so many lie dead.

I looked to heaven, and tried to pray ;
But or ever a prayer had gusht,
A wicked whisper came, and made
My heart as dry as dust.

I closed my lids, and kept them close,
And the balls like pulses beat ;
For the sky and the sea, and the sea and the
    sky
Lay like a load on my weary eye,
And the dead were at my feet.

But the
curse liveth
for him in
the eye of
the dead
men.

The cold sweat melted from their limbs,
Nor rot nor reek did they :
The look with which they looked on me
Has never passed away.

An orphan's curse would drag to hell
A spirit from on high ;
But oh ! more horrible than that
Is the curse in a dead man's eye !
Seven days, seven nights, I saw that curse,
And yet I could not die.

In his loneliness and
fixedness he yearneth
towards the journeying
Moon, and the stars that
still sojourn, yet still
move onward ; and every-
where the blue sky be-
longs to them, and is their
appointed rest, and their
native country and their
own natural homes, which
they enter unannounced,
as lords that are certainly
expected and yet there is
a silent joy at their arrival.

The moving Moon went up the sky,
And nowhere did abide :
Softly she was going up,
And a star or two beside—

Her beams bemocked the sultry
    main,
Like April hoar-frost spread ;
But where the ship's huge shadow
    lay,
The charmed water burnt alway
A still and awful red.

By the light
of the Moon
he beholdeth
God's crea-
tures of the
great calm.

Beyond the shadow of the ship,
I watched the water-snakes :
They moved in tracks of shining white,
And when they reared, the elfish light
Fell off in hoary flakes.

Within the shadow of the ship
I watched their rich attire :
Blue, glossy green, and velvet black,
They coiled and swam ; and every track
Was a flash of golden fire.

O happy living things ! no tongue
Their beauty might declare :
A spring of love gushed from my heart,
And I blessed them unaware :
Sure my kind saint took pity on me,
And I blessed them unaware.

Their beauty and their happiness.

He blesseth them in his heart.

The selfsame moment I could pray ;
And from my neck so free
The Albatross fell off, and sank
Like lead into the sea.

The spell begins to break.

PART V

Oh sleep ! it is a gentle thing,
Beloved from pole to pole !
To Mary Queen the praise be given !
She sent the gentle sleep from Heaven,
That slid into my soul.

The silly buckets on the deck,
That had so long remained,
I dreamt that they were filled with dew ;
And when I awoke, it rained.

By grace of the holy Mother, the ancient Mariner is refreshed with rain

My lips were wet, my throat was cold,
My garments all were dank ;
Sure I had drunken in my dreams,
And still my body drank.

I moved, and could not feel my limbs :
I was so light—almost
I thought that I had died in sleep,
And was a blessed ghost.

He heareth
sounds and
seeth strange
sights and
commotions
in the sky
and the
element.

And soon I heard a roaring wind :
⁻ did not come anear ;
ut with its sound it shook the sails,
That were so thin and sere.

The upper air burst into life !
And a hundred fire-flags sheen,
To and fro they were hurried about !
And to and fro, and in and out,
The wan stars danced between.

And the coming wind did roar more loud,
And the sails did sigh like sedge ;
And the rain poured down from one black
    cloud ;
The Moon was at its edge.

The thick black cloud was cleft, and still
The Moon was at its side :
Like waters shot from some high crag,
The lightning fell with never a jag,
A river steep and wide.

The bodies
of the ship's
crew are in-
spired, and
the ship
moves on ;

The loud wind never reached the ship,
Yet now the ship moved on !
Beneath the lightning and the Moon
The dead men gave a groan.

They groaned, they stirred, they all uprose,
Nor spake, nor moved their eyes ;
It had been strange, even in a dream,
To have seen those dead men rise.

56

COLERIDGE & HIS POETRY

The helmsman steered, the ship moved on ;
Yet never a breeze up blew ;
The mariners all 'gan work the ropes,
Where they were wont to do ;
They raised their limbs like lifeless tools—
We were a ghastly crew.

The bódy of my brother's son
Stood by me, knee to knee :
The body and I pulled at one rope
But he said nought to me.

" I fear thee, ancient Mariner ! "
Be calm, thou Wedding-Guest !
'Twas not those souls that fled in pain,
Which to their corses came again,
But a troop of spirits blest :

For when it dawned—they dropped their arms,
And clustered round the mast ;
Sweet sounds rose slowly through their mouths,
And from their bodies passed.

But not by
the souls of
the men, nor
by dæmons
of earth or
middle air,
but by a
blessed troop
of angelic
spirits, sent
down by the
invocation of
the guardian
saint.

Around, around, flew each sweet sound,
Then darted to the Sun ;
Slowly the sounds came back again,
Now mixed, now one by one.

Sometimes a-dropping from the sky
I heard the sky-lark sing ;
Sometimes all little birds that are,
How they seemed to fill the sea and air
With their sweet jargoning !

And now 'twas like all instruments,
Now like a lonely flute ;

57

And now it is an angel's song,
That makes the heavens be mute.

It ceased ; yet still the sails made on
A pleasant noise till noon,
A noise like of a hidden brook
In the leafy month of June,
That to the sleeping woods all night
Singeth a quiet tune.

Till noon we quietly sailed on,
Yet never a breeze did breathe :
Slowly and smoothly went the ship,
Moved onward from beneath.

The lonesome Spirit from the South Pole carries on the ship as far as the Line, in obedience to the angelic troop, but still requireth vengeance.

Under the keel nine fathom deep,
From the land of mist and snow,
The spirit slid : and it was he
That made the ship to go.
The sails at noon left off their tune,
And the ship stood still also.

The Sun, right up above the mast,
Had fixed her to the ocean :
But in a minute she 'gan stir,
With a short uneasy motion—
Backwards and forwards half her length
With a short uneasy motion.

Then like a pawing horse let go,
She made a sudden bound :
It flung the blood into my head,
And I fell down in a swound.

The Polar Spirit's fellow-dæmons, the invisible inhabitants of the element take part in his wrong ;

How long in that same fit I lay,
I have not to declare ;
But ere my living life returned,

I heard and in my soul discerned
Two voices in the air.

"Is it he?" quoth one, "Is this the
   man?
By him who died on cross,
With his cruel bow he laid full low
The harmless Albatross.

" The spirit who bideth by himself
In the land of mist and snow,
He loved the bird that loved the man
Who shot him with his bow."

The other was a softer voice,
As soft as honey-dew :
Quoth he, " The man hath penance done,
And penance more will do."

and two of them relate,
one to the other, that
penance long and heavy
for the ancient Mariner
hath been accorded to the
Polar Spirit, who return-
eth southward.

PART VI

FIRST VOICE

" But tell me, tell me ! speak again,
Thy soft response renewing—
What makes that ship drive on so fast ?
What is the ocean doing ? "

SECOND VOICE

" Still as a slave before his lord,
The ocean hath no blast ;
His great bright eye most silently
Up to the Moon is cast—

" If he may know which way to go ;
For she guides him smooth or grim.
See, brother, see ! how graciously
She looketh down on him."

59

COLERIDGE & HIS POETRY

The Mariner hath been cast into a trance ; for the angelic power causeth the vessel to drive northward faster than human life could endure.

" But why drives on that ship so fast,
Without or wave or wind ? "

SECOND VOICE

" The air is cut away before,
And closes from behind.

" Fly, brother, fly ! more high, more high !
Or we shall be belated :
For slow and slow that ship will go,
When the Mariner's trance is abated."

The super-natural motion is retarded; the Mariner awakes, and his penance begins anew.

I woke, and we were sailing on
As in a gentle weather :
'Twas night, calm night, the moon was high,
The dead men stood together.

All stood together on the deck,
For a charnel-dungeon fitter :
All fixed on me their stony eyes,
That in the Moon did glitter.

The pang, the curse, with which they died,
Had never passed away :
I could not draw my eyes from theirs,
Nor turn them up to pray.

The curse is finally ex-piated.

And now this spell was snapt : once more
I viewed the ocean green,
And looked far forth, yet little saw
Of what had else been seen—

Like one, that on a lonesome road
Doth walk in fear and dread,
60

And having once turned round walks on,
And turns no more his head ;
Because he knows, a frightful fiend
Doth close behind him tread.

But soon there breathed a wind on me,
Nor sound nor motion made :
Its path was not upon the sea,
In ripple or in shade.

It raised my hair, it fanned my cheek
Like a meadow-gale of spring—
It mingled strangely with my fears,
Yet it felt like a welcoming.

Swiftly, swiftly flew the ship,
Yet she sailed softly too :
Sweetly, sweetly blew the breeze—
On me alone it blew.

Oh ! dream of joy ! is this indeed
The lighthouse top I see ?
Is this the hill ? is this the kirk ?
Is this mine own countree ?

And the ancient Mariner beholdeth his native country.

We drifted o'er the harbour-bar,
And I with sobs did pray—
O let me be awake, my God !
Or let me sleep alway.

The harbour-bay was clear as glass,
So smoothly it was strewn !
And on the bay the moonlight lay,
And the shadow of the Moon.

The rock shone bright, the kirk no less,
That stands above the rock :

COLERIDGE & HIS POETRY

The moonlight steeped in silentness
The steady weathercock.

And the bay was white with silent light
Till rising from the same,
Full many shapes, that shadows were,
In crimson colours came.

The Angelic spirits leave the dead bodies,

And appear in their own forms of light.

A little distance from the prow
Those crimson shadows were :
I turned my eyes upon the deck—
Oh, Christ ! what saw I there !

Each corse lay flat, lifeless and flat,
And, by the holy rood !
A man all light, a seraph-man,
On every corse there stood.

This seraph-band, each waved his hand :
It was a heavenly sight !
They stood as signals to the land,
Each one a lovely light ;

This seraph-band, each waved his hand,
No voice did they impart—
No voice ; but oh ! the silence sank
Like music on my heart.

But soon I heard the dash of oars,
I heard the Pilot's cheer ;
My head was turned perforce away,
And I saw a boat appear.

The Pilot and the Pilot's boy,
I heard them coming fast :
Dear Lord in Heaven ! it was a joy
The dead men could not blast.

I saw a third—I heard his voice :
It is the Hermit good !
He singeth loud his godly hymns
That he makes in the wood.
He'll shrieve my soul, he'll wash away
The Albatross's blood.

PART VII

This Hermit good lives in that wood
Which slopes down to the sea.
How loudly his sweet voice he rears !
He loves to talk with marineres
That come from a far countree.

The Hermit of the Wood.

He kneels at morn, and noon, and eve—
He hath a cushion plump :
It is the moss that wholly hides
The rotted old oak-stump.

The skiff-boat neared : I heard them talk,
" Why, this is strange, I trow !
Where are those lights so many and fair,
That signal made but now ? "

" Strange, by my faith ! " the Hermit said—
" And they answered not our cheer !
The planks looked warped ! and see those sails,
How thin they are and sere !
I never saw aught like to them,
Unless perchance it were

Approacheth the ship with wonder.

" Brown skeletons of leaves that lag
My forest-brook along ;
When the ivy-tod is heavy with snow,
And the owlet whoops to the wolf below,
That eats the she-wolf's young."

" Dear Lord ! it hath a fiendish look "—
(The Pilot made reply)
" I am a-feared "—" Push on, push on ! "
Said the Hermit cheerily.

The boat came closer to the ship,
But I nor spake nor stirred ;
The boat came close beneath the ship,
And straight a sound was heard.

The ship
suddenly
sinketh.

Under the water it rumbled on,
Still louder and more dread :
It reached the ship, it split the bay ;
The ship went down like lead.

The ancient
Mariner is
saved in the
Pilot's boat.

Stunned by that loud and dreadful sound,
Which sky and ocean smote,
Like one that hath been seven days drowned
My body lay afloat ;
But swift as dreams, myself I found
Within the Pilot's boat.

Upon the whirl, where sank the ship,
The boat spun round and round ;
And all was still, save that the hill
Was telling of the sound.

I moved my lips—the Pilot shrieked
And fell down in a fit ;
The holy Hermit raised his eyes,
And prayed where he did sit.

I took the oars : the Pilot's boy,
Who now doth crazy go,
Laughed loud and long, and all the while
His eyes went to and fro.

"Ha! ha!" quoth he, "full plain I see,
The Devil knows how to row."

And now, all in my own countree,
I stood on the firm land!
The Hermit stepped forth from the boat,
And scarcely he could stand.

"O shrieve me, shrieve me, holy man!"
The Hermit crossed his brow.
"Say quick," quoth he, "I bid thee say—
What manner of man art thou?"

> The ancient Mariner earnestly entreateth the Hermit to shrieve him; and the penance of life falls on him.

Forthwith this frame of mine was wrenched
With a woful agony,
Which forced me to begin my tale;
And then it left me free.

Since then, at an uncertain hour,
That agony returns:
And till my ghastly tale is told,
This heart within me burns.

> And ever and anon throughout his future life an agony constraineth him to travel from land to land.

I pass, like night, from land to land;
I have strange power of speech;
That moment that his face I see,
I know the man that must hear me:
To him my tale I teach.

What loud uproar bursts from that door!
The wedding-guests are there:
But in the garden-bower the bride
And bride-maids singing are:
And hark the little vesper bell
Which biddeth me to prayer!

B

O Wedding-Guest ! this soul hath been
Alone on a wide wide sea :
So lonely 'twas, that God himself
Scarce seemed there to be.

O sweeter than the marriage-feast,
'Tis sweeter far to me,
To walk together to the kirk
With a goodly company !—

To walk together to the kirk,
And all together pray,
While each to his great Father bends,
Old men, and babes, and loving friends
And youths and maidens gay !

And to teach, by his own example, love and re-verence to all things that God made and loveth.

Farewell, farewell ! but this I tell
To thee, thou Wedding-Guest !
He prayeth well, who loveth well
Both man and bird and beast.

He prayeth best, who loveth best
All things both great and small ;
For the dear God who loveth us,
He made and loveth all.

The Mariner, whose eye is bright,
Whose beard with age is hoar,
Is gone : and now the Wedding-Guest
Turned from the bridegroom's door.

He went like one that hath been stunned,
And is of sense forlorn :
A sadder and a wiser man,
He rose the morrow morn.

66

Another aspect of the poem remains to be dealt with. Though Wordsworth and Coleridge approached their subjects from different points of view, in their feeling for Nature they constantly met on common ground. And, at this time of high emotions, of reawakened interest in life and living, the poets' feeling for Nature did not mean mere appreciation of her wonder and beauty. They looked on her, in her entirety, as an expression of the divine ; and in her organic whole all animated beings were one in fellowship. Thus their attitude to her was bound up with their philosophy, and was extended to active sympathy with all sentient creatures. "The Ancient Mariner" is permeated with a wide charity, a humanitarian spirit, which, in spite of Coleridge's deprecation of the attempt to read any particular lesson into it, makes it one of the most truly moral poems in our literature. In this respect it may be placed beside Wordsworth's "Hart-leap Well," the last verses of which afford an interesting parallel to the conclusion of Coleridge's poem.

Yet one more work taking us on to enchanted ground belongs to this wonderful year—Part I. of "Christabel." It was based, Coleridge said, on the idea that "the virtuous of this world save the wicked," but the scheme was destined never to be worked out. For "Christabel" remained a fragment, though a second part was written a few years later. But, complete or incomplete, it is not for moral, or even for meaning, that we read "Christabel." Its simple beauty—beauty of imagery, of melody, of mystery—captivates the imagination, while it defies analysis.

Here Coleridge, in revolt against the "classic" school, abandons himself to a free rhythm, which, as will be seen, depends entirely on the four accents in each line, while the number of syllables varies at will. This, in itself significant, gives free play to the poet's power over the melody of verse, and seldom, if ever elsewhere, has verse been set to such witching music. We have an ancient castle, a wood at night, moonlight, oppressive silence—all the romantic machinery of the supernatural. But the appeals to the imagination are made by the subtlest suggestions ; the sources of terror are not sought in material horrors ; the supernatural is never pushed over the borders of psychologic truth. In imagery and allegory Spenser's influence may be traced. Coleridge attempts and achieves in Part II. a feat that has been described as " the most difficult of execution in the whole field of romance "—enchantment by daylight. This part was probably written about 1800 ; it is reproduced here with Part I.

CHRISTABEL
PART THE FIRST

'Tis the middle of night by the castle clock,
And the owls have awakened the crowing cock,
Tu—whit !——Tu—whoo !
And hark, again ! the crowing cock,
How drowsily it crew.

COLERIDGE & HIS POETRY

Sir Leoline, the Baron rich,
Hath a toothless mastiff, which
From her kennel beneath the rock
Maketh answer to the clock,
Four for the quarters, and twelve for the hour ;
Ever and aye, by shine and shower,
Sixteen short howls, not over loud ;
Some say, she sees my lady's shroud.

Is the night chilly and dark ?
The night is chilly, but not dark.
The thin gray cloud is spread on high,
It covers but not hides the sky.
The moon is behind, and at the full ;
And yet she looks both small and dull.
The night is chill, the cloud is gray :
'Tis a month before the month of May,
And the Spring comes slowly up this way.

The lovely lady, Christabel,
Whom her father loves so well,
What makes her in the wood so late,
A furlong from the castle gate ?
She had dreams all yesternight
Of her own betrothed knight ;
And she in the midnight wood will pray
For the weal of her lover that's far away.

She stole along, she nothing spoke,
The sighs she heaved were soft and low,
And nought was green upon the oak
But moss and rarest mistletoe :
She kneels beneath the huge oak tree,
And in silence prayeth she.

The lady sprang up suddenly,
The lovely lady, Christabel !
It moaned as near, as near can be,
But what it is she cannot tell.—
On the other side it seems to be,
Of the huge, broad-breasted, old oak tree.

The night is chill ; the forest bare ;
Is it the wind that moaneth bleak ?
There is not wind enough in the air
To move away the ringlet curl
From the lovely lady's cheek—

There is not wind enough to twirl
The one red leaf, the last of its clan,
That dances as often as dance it can,
Hanging so light, and hanging so high,
On the topmost twig that looks up at the sky.

Hush, beating heart of Christabel !
Jesu, Maria, shield her well !
She folded her arms beneath her cloak,
And stole to the other side of the oak.
    What sees she there ?

There she sees a damsel bright,
Drest in a silken robe of white,
That shadowy in the moonlight shone :
The neck that made that white robe wan,
Her stately neck, and arms were bare ;
Her blue-veined feet unsandal'd were,
And wildly glittered here and there
The gems entangled in her hair.
I guess, 'twas frightful there to see
A lady so richly clad as she—
Beautiful exceedingly !

Mary mother, save me now !
(Said Christabel,) And who art thou ?

The lady strange made answer meet,
And her voice was faint and sweet : —
Have pity on my sore distress,
I scarce can speak for weariness :
Stretch forth thy hand, and have no fear !
Said Christabel, How camest thou here ?
And the lady, whose voice was faint and sweet,
Did thus pursue her answer meet : —

My sire is of a noble line,
And my name is Geraldine :
Five warriors seized me yestermorn,
Me, even me, a maid forlorn :
They choked my cries with force and fright,
And tied me on a palfrey white.
The palfrey was as fleet as wind,
And they rode furiously behind.
They spurred amain, their steeds were white :
And once we crossed the shade of night.
As sure as Heaven shall rescue me,
I have no thought what men they be ;
Nor do I know how long it is
(For I have lain entranced I wis)
Since one, the tallest of the five,
Took me from the palfrey's back,
A weary woman, scarce alive.
Some muttered words his comrades spoke :
He placed me underneath this oak ;
He swore they would return with haste ;
Whither they went I cannot tell—
I thought I heard, some minutes past,
Sounds as of a castle bell.

Stretch forth thy hand (thus ended she),
And help a wretched maid to flee.

Then Christabel stretched forth her hand,
And comforted fair Geraldine :
O well, bright dame ! may you command
The service of Sir Leoline ;
And gladly our stout chivalry
Will he send forth and friends withal
To guide and guard you safe and free
Home to your noble father's hall.

She rose : and forth with steps they passed
That strove to be, and were not, fast.
Her gracious stars the lady blest,
And thus spake on sweet Christabel :
All our household are at rest,
The hall as silent as the cell ;
Sir Leoline is weak in health,
And may not well awakened be,
But we will move as if in stealth,
And I beseech your courtesy,
This night, to share your couch with me.

They crossed the moat, and Christabel
Took the key that fitted well ;
A little door she opened straight,
All in the middle of the gate ;
The gate that was ironed within and without,
Where an army in battle array had marched out.
The lady sank, belike through pain,
And Christabel with might and main
Lifted her up, a weary weight,
Over the threshold of the gate :
Then the lady rose again,
And moved, as she were not in pain.

So free from danger, free from fear,
They crossed the court : right glad they were.
And Christabel devoutly cried
To the lady by her side,
Praise we the Virgin all divine
Who hath rescued thee from thy distress !
Alas, alas ! said Geraldine,
I cannot speak for weariness.
So free from danger, free from fear,
They crossed the court : right glad they were.

Outside her kennel, the mastiff old
Lay fast asleep, in moonshine cold.
The mastiff old did not awake,
Yet she an angry moan did make !
And what can ail the mastiff bitch ?
Never till now she uttered yell
Beneath the eye of Christabel.
Perhaps it is the owlet's scritch :
For what can ail the mastiff bitch ?

They passed the hall, that echoes still,
Pass as lightly as you will !
The brands were flat, the brands were dying,
Amid their own white ashes lying ;
But when the lady passed, there came
A tongue of light, a fit of flame ;
And Christabel saw the lady's eye,
And nothing else saw she thereby,
Save the boss of the shield of Sir Leoline tall,
Which hung in a murky old niche in the wall.
O softly tread, said Christabel,
My father seldom sleepeth well.

Sweet Christabel her feet doth bare,
And jealous of the listening air
They steal their way from stair to stair,
Now in glimmer, and now in gloom,
And now they pass the Baron's room,
As still as death, with stifled breath !
And now have reached her chamber door ;
And now doth Geraldine press down
The rushes of the chamber floor.

The moon shines dim in the open air,
And not a moonbeam enters here.
But they without its light can see
The chamber carved so curiously,
Carved with figures strange and sweet,
All made out of the carver's brain,
For a lady's chamber meet :
The lamp with twofold silver chain
Is fastened to an angel's feet.

The silver lamp burns dead and dim ;
But Christabel the lamp will trim.
She trimmed the lamp, and made it bright,
And left it swinging to and fro,
While Geraldine, in wretched plight,
Sank down upon the floor below.

O weary lady, Geraldine,
I pray you, drink this cordial wine !
It is a wine of virtuous powers ;
My mother made it of wild flowers.

And will your mother pity me,
Who am a maiden most forlorn ?
Christabel answered Woe is me !
She died the hour that I was born.

I have heard the grey-haired friar tell
How on her death-bed she did say,
That she should hear the castle-bell
Strike twelve upon my wedding-day.
O mother dear ! that thou wert here !
I would, said Geraldine, she were !

But soon with altered voice, said she—
" Off, wandering mother !   Peak and pine !
I have power to bid thee flee."
Alas ! what ails poor Geraldine ?
Why stares she with unsettled eye ?
Can she the bodiless dead espy ?
And why with hollow voice cries she,
" Off, woman, off ! this hour is mine—
Though thou her guardian spirit be,
Off, woman, off ! 'tis given to me."

Then Christabel knelt by the lady's side,
And raised to heaven her eyes so blue—
Alas ! said she, this ghastly ride—
Dear lady ! it hath wildered you !
The lady wiped her moist cold brow,
And faintly said, " 'Tis over now ! "

Again the wild-flower wine she drank :
Her fair large eyes 'gan glitter bright,
And from the floor whereon she sank,
The lofty lady stood upright :
She was most beautiful to see,
Like a lady of a far countree.

And thus the lofty lady spake—
" All they who live in the upper sky,
Do love you, holy Christabel !
And you love them, and for their sake

And for the good which me befel,
Even I in my degree will try,
Fair maiden, to requite you well.
But now unrobe yourself ; for I
Must pray, ere yet in bed I lie.''

Quoth Christabel, So let it be !
And as the lady bade, did she.
Her gentle limbs did she undress,
And lay down in her loveliness.

But through her brain of weal and woe
So many thoughts moved to and fro,
That vain it were her lids to close ;
So half-way from the bed she rose,
And on her elbow did recline
To look at the lady Geraldine.

Beneath the lamp the lady bowed,
And slowly rolled her eyes around ;
Then drawing in her breath aloud,
Like one that shuddered, she unbound
The cincture from beneath her breast :
Her silken robe, and inner vest,
Dropt to her feet, and full in view,
Behold ! her bosom and half her side—
A sight to dream of, not to tell !
O shield her ! shield sweet Christabel !

Yet Geraldine nor speaks nor stirs ;
Ah ! what a stricken look was hers !
Deep from within she seems half-way
To lift some weight with sick assay,
And eyes the maid and seeks delay ;

Then suddenly, as one defied,
Collects herself in scorn and pride,
And lay down by the Maiden's side !—
And in her arms the maid she took,
    Ah well-a-day !
And with low voice and doleful look
These words did say :

"In the touch of this bosom there worketh a spell,
Which is lord of thy utterance, Christabel !
Thou knowest to-night, and wilt know to-morrow,
This mark of my shame, this seal of my sorrow ;
    But vainly thou warrest,
     For this is alone in
    Thy power to declare,
     That in the dim forest
    Thou heard'st a low moaning,
And found'st a bright lady, surpassingly fair ;
And didst bring her home with thee in love and in
   charity,
To shield her and shelter her from the damp air."

THE CONCLUSION TO PART THE FIRST

It was a lovely sight to see
The lady Christabel, when she
Was praying at the old oak tree.
    Amid the jagged shadows
    Of mossy leafless boughs,
    Kneeling in the moonlight,
    To make her gentle vows ;
Her slender palms together prest,
Heaving sometimes on her breast ;

Her face resigned to bliss or bale—
Her face, oh call it fair not pale,
And both blue eyes more bright than clear,
Each about to have a tear.

With open eyes (ah woe is me !)
Asleep, and dreaming fearfully,
Fearfully dreaming, yet, I wis,
Dreaming that alone, which is—
O sorrow and shame ! Can this be she,
The lady, who knelt at the old oak tree ?
And lo ! the worker of these harms,
That holds the maiden in her arms,
Seems to slumber still and mild,
As a mother with her child.

A star hath set, a star hath risen,
O Geraldine ! since arms of thine
Have been the lovely lady's prison.
O Geraldine ! one hour was thine—
Thou'st had thy will ! By tairn and rill,
The night-birds all that hour were still.
But now they are jubilant anew,
From cliff and tower, tu—whoo ! tu—whoo !
Tu—whoo ! tu—whoo ! from wood and fell !

And see ! the lady Christabel
Gathers herself from out her trance ;
Her limbs relax, her countenance
Grows sad and soft ; the smooth thin lids
Close o'er her eyes ; and tears she sheds—
Large tears that leave the lashes bright !
And oft the while she seems to smile
As infants at a sudden light !

Yea, she doth smile, and she doth weep,
Like a youthful hermitess,
Beauteous in a wilderness,
Who, praying always, prays in sleep.
And, if she move unquietly,
Perchance, 'tis but the blood so free
Comes back and tingles in her feet.
No doubt, she hath a vision sweet.

What if her guardian spirit 'twere,
What if she knew her mother near ?
But this she knows, in joys and woes,
That saints will aid if men will call :
For the blue sky bends over all !

PART THE SECOND

Each matin bell, the Baron saith,
Knells us back to a world of death.
These words Sir Leoline first said,
When he rose and found his lady dead :
These words Sir Leoline will say
Many a morn to his dying day !

And hence the custom and law began
That still at dawn the sacristan,
Who duly pulls the heavy bell,
Five and forty beads must tell
Between each stroke—a warning knell,
Which not a soul can choose but hear
From Bratha Head to Wyndermere.

Saith Bracy the bard, So let it knell !
And let the drowsy sacristan
Still count as slowly as he can !

There is no lack of such, I ween,
As well fill up the space between.
In Langdale Pike and Witch's Lair,
And Dungeon-ghyll so foully rent,
With ropes of rock and bells of air
Three sinful sextons' ghosts are pent,
Who all give back, one after t'other,
The death-note to their living brother ;
And oft too, by the knell offended,
Just as their one ! two ! three ! is ended,
The devil mocks the doleful tale
With a merry peal from Borrowdale.

The air is still ! through mist and cloud
That merry peal comes ringing loud ;
And Geraldine shakes off her dread,
And rises lightly from the bed ;
Puts on her silken vestments white,
And tricks her hair in lovely plight,
And nothing doubting of her spell
Awakens the lady Christabel.
" Sleep you, sweet lady Christabel ?
I trust that you have rested well.''

And Christabel awoke and spied
The same who lay down by her side—
O rather say, the same whom she
Raised up beneath the old oak tree !
Nay, fairer yet ! and yet more fair !
For she belike hath drunken deep
Of all the blessedness of sleep !
And while she spake, her looks, her air,
Such gentle thankfulness declare,
That (so it seemed) her girded vests
Grew tight beneath her heaving breasts.

" Sure I have sinn'd ! " said Christabel,
" Now heaven be praised if all be well ! "
And in low faltering tones, yet sweet,
Did she the lofty lady greet
With such perplexity of mind
As dreams too lively leave behind.

So quickly she rose, and quickly arrayed
Her maiden limbs, and having prayed
That He, who on the cross did groan,
Might wash away her sins unknown,
She forthwith led fair Geraldine
To meet her sire, Sir Leoline.

The lovely maid and the lady tall
Are pacing both into the hall,
And pacing on through page and groom,
Enter the Baron's presence-room.

The Baron rose, and while he prest
His gentle daughter to his breast,
With cheerful wonder in his eyes
The lady Geraldine espies,
And gave such welcome to the same,
As might beseem so bright a dame !

But when he heard the lady's tale,
And when she told her father's name,
Why waxed Sir Leoline so pale,
Murmuring o'er the name again,
Lord Roland de Vaux of Tryermaine ?

Alas ! they had been friends in youth ;
But whispering tongues can poison truth ;
And constancy lives in realms above ;
And life is thorny ; and youth is vain ;

And to be wroth with one we love
Doth work like madness in the brain.
And thus it chanced, as I divine,
With Roland and Sir Leoline.

Each spake words of high disdain
And insult to his heart's best brother :
They parted—ne'er to meet again !
But never either found another
To free the hollow heart from paining—
They stood aloof, the scars remaining,
Like cliffs which had been rent asunder ;
A dreary sea now flows between.
But neither heat, nor frost, nor thunder,
Shall wholly do away, I ween,
The marks of that which once hath been.

Sir Leoline, a moment's space,
Stood gazing on the damsel's face :
And the youthful Lord of Tryermaine
Came back upon his heart again.

O then the Baron forgot his age,
His noble heart swelled high with rage ;
He swore by the wounds in Jesu's side
He would proclaim it far and wide,
With trump and solemn heraldry,
That they, who thus had wronged the dame
Were base as spotted infamy !
" And if they dare deny the same,
My herald shall appoint a week,
And let the recreant traitors seek
My tourney court—that there and then
I may dislodge their reptile souls
From the bodies and forms of men ! "
He spake : his eye in lightning rolls !

For the lady was ruthlessly seized ; and he kenned
In the beautiful lady the child of his friend !

And now the tears were on his face,
And fondly in his arms he took
Fair Geraldine, who met the embrace,
Prolonging it with joyous look.
Which when she viewed, a vision fell
Upon the soul of Christabel,
The vision of fear, the touch and pain !
She shrunk and shuddered, and saw again—
(Ah, woe is me ! Was it for thee,
Thou gentle maid ! such sights to see ?)

Again she saw that bosom old,
Again she felt that bosom cold,
And drew in her breath with a hissing sound :
Whereat the Knight turned wildly round,
And nothing saw, but his own sweet maid
With eyes upraised, as one that prayed.

The touch, the sight, had passed away,
And in its stead that vision blest,
Which comforted her after-rest,
While in the lady's arms she lay,
Had put a rapture in her breast,
And on her lips and o'er her eyes
Spread smiles like light !
               With new surprise,
" What ails then my beloved child ? "
The Baron said—His daughter mild
Made answer, " All will yet be well ! "
I ween, she had no power to tell
Aught else : so mighty was the spell.
Yet he, who saw this Geraldine,
Had deemed her sure a thing divine.

Such sorrow with such grace she blended,
And if she feared she had offended
Sweet Christabel, that gentle maid !
And with such lowly tones she prayed
She might be sent without delay
Home to her father's mansion.

                     " Nay !
Nay, by my soul ! " said Leoline.
" Ho !   Bracy the bard, the charge be thine !
Go thou, with music sweet and loud,
And take two steeds with trappings proud,
And take the youth whom thou lov'st best
To bear thy harp, and learn thy song,
And clothe you both in solemn vest,
And over the mountains haste along,
Lest wandering folk, that are abroad,
Detain you on the valley road.

" And when he has crossed the Irthing flood,
My merry bard ! he hastes, he hastes
Up Knorren Moor, through Halegarth Wood,
And reaches soon that castle good
Which stands and threatens Scotland's wastes.

" Bard Bracy ! bard Bracy ! your horses are fleet,
Ye must ride up the hall, your music so sweet,
More loud than your horses' echoing feet !
And loud and loud to Lord Roland call,
Thy daughter is safe in Langdale hall !
Thy beautiful daughter is safe and free—
Sir Leoline greets thee thus through me.
He bids thee come without delay
With all thy numerous array ;
And take thy lovely daughter home :
And he will meet thee on the way

With all his numerous array
White with their panting palfreys' foam :
And, by mine honour ! I will say,
That I repent me of the day
When I spake words of fierce disdain
To Roland de Vaux of Tryermaine !—
—For since that evil hour hath flown,
Many a summer's sun hath shone ;
Yet ne'er found I a friend again
Like Roland de Vaux of Tryermaine."

The lady fell, and clasped his knees,
Her face upraised, her eyes o'erflowing ;
And Bracy replied, with faltering voice,
His gracious hail on all bestowing ;
" Thy words, thou sire of Christabel,
Are sweeter than my harp can tell ;
Yet might I gain a boon of thee,
This day my journey should not be,
So strange a dream hath come to me ;
That I had vowed with music loud
To clear yon wood from thing unblest,
Warn'd by a vision in my rest !
For in my sleep I saw that dove,
That gentle bird, whom thou dost love,
And call'st by thy own daughter's name—
Sir Leoline ! I saw the same,
Fluttering, and uttering fearful moan,
Among the green herbs in the forest alone.
Which when I saw and when I heard,
I wonder'd what might ail the bird ;
For nothing near it could I see,
Save the grass and green herbs underneath the
    old tree.

" And in my dream, methought, I went
To search out what might there be found ;
And what the sweet bird's trouble meant,
That thus lay fluttering on the ground.
I went and peered, and could descry
No cause for her distressful cry ;
But yet for her dear lady's sake
I stooped, methought, the dove to take,
When lo ! I saw a bright green snake
Coiled around its wings and neck,
Green as the herbs on which it couched,
Close by the dove's its head it crouched ;
And with the dove it heaves and stirs,
Swelling its neck as she swelled hers !
I woke ; it was the midnight hour,
The clock was echoing in the tower ;
But though my slumber was gone by,
This dream it would not pass away—
It seems to live upon my eye !
And thence I vowed this self-same day
With music strong and saintly song
To wander through the forest bare,
Lest aught unholy loiter there.''

Thus Bracy said : the Baron, the while,
Half-listening heard him with a smile ;
Then turned to Lady Geraldine,
His eyes made up of wonder and love ;
And said in courtly accents fine,
" Sweet maid, Lord Roland's beauteous dove,
With arms more strong than harp or song,
Thy sire and I will crush the snake ! ''
He kissed her forehead as he spake,
And Geraldine in maiden wise
Casting down her large bright eyes,

With blushing cheek and courtesy fine
She turned her from Sir Leoline ;
Softly gathering up her train,
That o'er her right arm fell again ;
And folded her arms across her chest,
And couched her head upon her breast,
And looked askance at Christabel——
Jesu, Maria, shield her well !

A snake's small eye blinks dull and shy,
And the lady's eyes they shrunk in her head,
Each shrunk up to a serpent's eye,
And with somewhat of malice, and more of dread,
At Christabel she look'd askance !—
One moment—and the sight was fled !
But Christabel in dizzy trance
Stumbling on the unsteady ground
Shuddered aloud, with a hissing sound ;
And Geraldine again turned round,
And like a thing, that sought relief,
Full of wonder and full of grief,
She rolled her large bright eyes divine
Wildly on Sir Leoline.

The maid, alas ! her thoughts are gone,
She nothing sees—no sight but one !
The maid, devoid of guile and sin,
I know not how, in fearful wise,
So deeply had she drunken in
That look, those shrunken serpent eyes,
That all her features were resigned
To this sole image in her mind :
And passively did imitate
That look of dull and treacherous hate !
And thus she stood, in dizzy trance,
Still picturing that look askance

With forced unconscious sympathy
Full before her father's view——
As far as such a look could be
In eyes so innocent and blue !

And when the trance was o'er, the maid
Paused awhile, and inly prayed :
Then falling at the Baron's feet,
" By my mother's soul do I entreat
That thou this woman send away ! "
She said : and more she could not say :
For what she knew she could not tell,
O'er-mastered by the mighty spell.

Why is thy cheek so wan and wild,
Sir Leoline ?   Thy only child
Lies at thy feet, thy joy, thy pride,
So fair, so innocent, so mild ;
The same, for whom thy lady died !
O, by the pangs of her dear mother
Think thou no evil of thy child !
For her, and thee, and for no other,
She prayed the moment ere she died :
Prayed that the babe for whom she died,
Might prove her dear lord's joy and pride !
    That prayer her deadly pangs beguiled,
        Sir Leoline !
    And wouldst thou wrong thy only child,
        Her child and thine ?

Within the Baron's heart and brain
If thoughts, like these, had any share,
They only swelled his rage and pain,
And did but work confusion there.
His heart was cleft with pain and rage,
His cheeks they quivered, his eyes were wild,

Dishonour'd thus in his old age ;
Dishonour'd by his only child,
And all his hospitality
To the insulted daughter of his friend
By more than woman's jealousy
Brought thus to a disgraceful end—
He rolled his eye with stern regard
Upon the gentle minstrel bard,
And said in tones abrupt, austere—
" Why, Bracy ! dost thou loiter here ?
I bade thee hence ! " The bard obeyed ;
And turning from his own sweet maid,
The aged knight, Sir Leoline,
Led forth the lady Geraldine !

THE CONCLUSION TO PART THE SECOND

A little child, a limber elf,
Singing, dancing to itself,
A fairy thing with red round cheeks,
That always finds, and never seeks,
Makes such a vision to the sight
As fills a father's eyes with light ;
And pleasures flow in so thick and fast
Upon his heart, that he at last
Must needs express his love's excess
With words of unmeant bitterness.

Perhaps 'tis pretty to force together
Thoughts so all unlike each other ;
To mutter and mock a broken charm,
To dally with wrong that does no harm.
Perhaps 'tis tender too and pretty
At each wild word to feel within
A sweet recoil of love and pity.
And what, if in a world of sin

COLERIDGE & HIS POETRY

(O sorrow and shame should this be true !]
Such giddiness of heart and brain
Comes seldom save from rage and pain,
So talks as it's most used to do.

Two passages in the second part are unsurpassed—one, the beautiful lines on broken
friendship beginning " Alas ! they had been
friends in youth " ; and the other the wonderful description of the spell cast by Geraldine over
Christabel. It was the first of these that recon-
ciled Lamb to the continuation of the poem.
He had resisted it, fearing it could not be main-
tained at the high level of Part I., and he told
the Gillmans, " I was very angry with Coleridge
when first I heard that he had written a second
canto, and that he intended to finish it ; but
when I read the beautiful apostrophe of the two
friends it calmed me." Perhaps Coleridge was
thinking of his disagreement with Southey over
the Pantisocracy when he wrote the lines.

On hearing the passage depicting Christabel's
dumb agony of helplessness under Geraldine's
" serpent's eye," Shelley is said to have fainted.
Here, as in Part I., the description is not so
much of the sight Christabel beholds, as of its
effect on her, and thus it takes possession of
the imagination with a sense of horror all the
stronger from its vagueness.

How Coleridge intended to complete the poem
is not really known. For years he was anxious
to do so, but the inspiration for which he waited
never came. To achieve that which he aimed

at achieving in depicting the supernatural, it needs no conclusion. In its incompleteness it touches perfection. Yet when a publisher undertook to publish it, in 1816, at Byron's instigation, there was still found a critic of weight to greet it as " utterly destitute of value, exhibiting from beginning to end not one ray of genius."

Scott, who heard it recited soon after it was written, was so charmed by the music of the rhythm that he adopted it for his " Lay of the Last Minstrel."

To the magic heights on which he trod in " Christabel," the fairy seas sailed in the " Ancient Mariner," Coleridge never again found the way. He soared there once on rapid pinion. Henceforth his muse was hampered with trailing wing. That he was largely responsible, as it may be urged, for the causes which combined to bring this about, does not lessen the tragedy or diminish the loss.

V

This year of his most brilliant achievement did not pass for Coleridge untroubled. The dream with which he had gone to Nether Stowey, of supporting a growing family on the products of the garden, and the money received for occasional poems, soon proved itself utterly impracticable. A second edition of his poems in 1797 brought only a little temporary aid. A difference with Lloyd led to his departure and the loss of the income he brought with him. A tragedy, "Osorio," written to get money, was rejected by the Drury Lane Committee, though some years later it was accepted, on Byron's recommendation, under the title "Remorse," and had a successful run. Coleridge again, therefore, felt the necessity of finding some permanent means of livelihood. And again, face to face with a practical problem, he showed great irresolution, giving way to depression when what was required was action. He wrote to Cottle, who had visited Stowey, and gone away ready to make further efforts and sacrifices on his behalf : "A sort of calm hopelessness diffuses itself over my heart. Indeed, every mode of life which has promised me bread and cheese has been, one after another, torn away from me." The assistance given him by Poole could not permanently solve the problem.

Meanwhile another cause contributed to unsettle him. Owing, tradition says, to a suspicion that got about that Wordsworth and Coleridge were dangerous characters, plotting against the Government, the owner of Alfoxden refused to let it to the Wordsworths after the Midsummer of 1798. The Wordsworths were uncertain where to settle. No place could be found in the neighbourhood, and thus an end was threatened to the delightful intercourse that had meant so much to all.

It was under these circumstances that Coleridge, already known in Unitarian pulpits, considered the acceptance of an offer that was made him of the post of Unitarian minister at Shrewsbury. Here, at the beginning of 1798, Hazlitt saw him for the first time, walking the ten miles in to Shrewsbury in order to hear him preach. He has given an account of his first impressions. As Coleridge gave out his text, he says, his voice " rose like a steam of rich distilled perfumes. . . . The preacher then launched into his subject like an eagle dallying with the wind. . . . And for myself, I could not have been more delighted if I had heard the music of the spheres. Poetry and Philosophy had met together, Truth and Genius had embraced, under the eye and with the sanction of Religion."

Two days later Coleridge visited Hazlitt's father. In recollections written years after Hazlitt thus describes him as he appeared to him then : " His forehead was broad and high, light as if built of ivory, with large projecting eyebrows, and his eyes rolling beneath them like a sea with darkened lustre. . . . His mouth was gross, voluptuous, open, eloquent ; his chin good-humoured and round ; but his nose, the rudder of the face, the index of the will, was small, feeble, nothing—like what he has done. It might seem that the genius of his face as from a height surveyed and projected him (with sufficient capacity and huge aspiration) into the world unknown of thought and imagination, with nothing to support or guide his veering purpose, as if Columbus had launched his adventurous course for the New World in a

scallop without oars or compass. So at least
I comment on it after the event." When he
left, Hazlitt accompanied him six miles on his
road. "The scholar in Chaucer is described
as going—'Sounding on his way.' So Coleridge
went on his. In digressing, in dilating, in
passing from subject to subject, he appeared to
me to float in air, to slide on ice. . . . I had
heard a great deal of his powers of conversation
and was not disappointed. In fact, I never met
with anything at all like them, either before or
since."

But before he left Shrewsbury Coleridge had
received and accepted an offer which, for good
or ill, relieved him of the pressing necessity of
undertaking the ministry, or looking further
for any practical means of earning his livelihood. One of the visitors to Nether Stowey in
1797 was a friend of Poole's, Thomas Wedgwood, son of the famous potter. He had come
quickly under the spell of Coleridge's genius,
and believed him capable of great things. He
and his brother, Josiah Wedgwood, were
possessors of what Josiah described in a letter
to Coleridge as "a considerable superfluity of
fortune," which they held "rather as Trustees
than as Proprietors" and were "earnestly
desirous to convert . . . into a fund of bene-
ficence." With this in view they now came
forward to offer Coleridge "an annuity for life
of £150 to be regularly paid by us, no condition
whatsoever being annexed to it." And of this
"unexampled liberality" Coleridge soon decided

to take advantage, believing, no doubt, that, free from the " touch of the hand of obligation," his genius, which he told himself was always hampered by necessity, would be able to give to the world something worthy of the confidence thus shown in him.

The immediate result of the security thus afforded him was to enable him to undertake a long-desired journey to Germany with the Wordsworths, with the idea, at least on Coleridge's part, of studying the language, literature, and philosophy of that country. They set out, accompanied by a young Stowey friend, John Chester, in September 1798, just after the publication of the " Lyrical Ballads," which Mrs. Coleridge was soon to report to them as " not liked at all by any." After a visit to the poet Klopstock at Hamburg, Coleridge and the Wordsworths parted, Coleridge going to stay with a pastor at Ratzeburg, determined " to acquire a thorough knowledge of German." For four months he worked really hard there ; then he went on to the University of Göttingen, equipped to pursue his studies. Here he found some other young English students, Carrlyon and Parry, who have recorded the impressions he made on them and his manner of living. The picture they give shows him full of energy and enthusiasm ; interested in a wide—indeed Parry suggests, significantly, a too wide—range of subjects ; entering into the social life of students and professors ; charming by his eloquence, mystifying by his philosophical speculations. Soon Coleridge reports to Josiah Wedgwood that he has learned " both high and low German," and can speak high German fluently, " but my pronunciation is hideous." Many other studies also have occupied him, and at least two great projects have taken possession of his mind—a History of the Belles-Lettres in Germany before the time of Lessing, and a life of Lessing—neither of them ever to be carried out. Yet what he did achieve during his nine months or so abroad must have demanded real concentration and hard work. Besides learning the language and studying literature, he drank deeply of German philosophy. And it was as a philosopher that he afterwards became " the interpreter of Germany to England." For though, as we shall see, various other causes nothing to do with his travels go to explain it, and though Germany did not make a metaphysician of him—he had been that from a schoolboy—his stay there coincides, with very few exceptions later, with his death as a poet.

His letters to his wife from abroad were full of affection and longing for home ; and to the desire to get back was added tender anxiety for Hartley, roused when he heard of the death of Berkeley, his second son, a baby of nine months old. On his return to England, in July 1799, he went straight to Stowey. But the Wordsworths were no longer near and he did not stay there. After a tour with Wordsworth and his brother in the Lake district, where Wordsworth

96

and Dorothy soon settled, Coleridge went to London, and accepted an engagement on the "Morning Post," a paper to which he had contributed poems frequently during the Stowey period. He now undertook to contribute political articles; he consequently stayed in London and the cottage at Stowey was given up.

It was probably while he was with the Wordsworths that Coleridge wrote the poem entitled "Love," published as "Introduction to the 'Tale of the Dark Ladie,'" which itself remained a fragment. If it was at this time "Love" was written, it was a swan-song to the period of happiness, love, and inspiration to which, in leaving Stowey for Germany, he bade farewell. Here once more there is delicacy of imagination, weaving together nature and human emotion; exquisite melody; and tenderness of feeling.

LOVE

All thoughts, all passions, all delights,
Whatever stirs this mortal frame,
All are but ministers of Love,
    And feed his sacred flame.

Oft in my waking dreams do I
Live o'er again that happy hour,
When midway on the mount I lay,
    Beside the ruined tower.

The moonshine, stealing o'er the scene
Had blended with the lights of eve;
And she was there, my hope, my joy,
    My own dear Genevieve!

G

She leant against the armed man,
The statue of the armed knight ;
She stood and listened to my lay,
    Amid the lingering light.

Few sorrows hath she of her own.
My hope ! my joy ! my Genevieve !
She loves me best, whene'er I sing
    The songs that make her grieve.

I played a soft and doleful air,
I sang an old and moving story—
An old rude song, that suited well
    That ruin wild and hoary.

She listened with a flitting blush,
With downcast eyes and modest grace ;
For well she knew, I could not choose
    But gaze upon her face.

I told her of the knight that wore
Upon his shield a burning brand ;
And that for ten long years he wooed
    The Lady of the Land.

I told her how he pined : and ah !
The deep, the low, the pleading tone
With which I sang another's love,
    Interpreted my own.

She listened with a flitting blush,
With downcast eyes, and modest grace
And she forgave me, that I gazed
    Too fondly on her face !

But when I told the cruel scorn
That crazed that bold and lovely Knight,
And that he crossed the mountain-woods,
    Nor rested day nor night ;

That sometimes from the savage den,
And sometimes from the darksome shade
And sometimes starting up at once
    In green and sunny glade,—

There came and looked him in the face
An angel beautiful and bright ;
And that he knew it was a Fiend,
    This miserable Knight !

And that unknowing what he did,
He leaped amid a murderous band,
And saved from outrage worse than death
    The Lady of the Land !

And how she wept, and clasped his knees ;
And how she tended him in vain—
And ever strove to expiate
    The scorn that crazed his brain ;—

And that she nursed him in a cave ;
And how his madness went away,
When on the yellow forest-leaves
    A dying man he lay ;—

His dying words—but when I reached
That tenderest strain of all the ditty,
My faltering voice and pausing harp
    Disturbed her soul with pity !

All impulses of soul and sense
Had thrilled my guileless Genevieve ;
The music and the doleful tale,
    The rich and balmy eve ;

And hopes, and fears that kindle hope,
An undistinguishable throng,
And gentle wishes long subdued,
    Subdued and cherished long !

She wept with pity and delight,
She blushed with love, and virgin-shame ;
And like the murmur of a dream,
    I heard her breathe my name.

Her bosom heaved—she stepped aside,
As conscious of my look she stepped—
Then suddenly, with timorous eye
    She fled to me and wept.

She half enclosed me with her arms,
She pressed me with a meek embrace ;
And bending back her head, looked up,
    And gazed upon my face.

'Twas partly love, and partly fear,
And partly 'twas a bashful art,
That I might rather feel, than see,
    The swelling of her heart.

I calmed her fears, and she was calm,
And told her love with virgin pride ;
And so I won my Genevieve,
    My bright and beauteous Bride.

COLERIDGE & HIS POETRY

When Coleridge returned from Germany he had, to all appearances, almost everything in his favour. He was freed from pressing money anxieties ; the happiness of his home was as yet unimpaired ; he was young ; he had had a bright, brief period of supreme achievement ; in Germany he had shown energy and concentration. Everything seemed to point to a brilliant future. Yet the period which followed was one in which hardly one projected plan was brought to completion ; it was a period of unfulfilled promise, of dissipated energies, of drifting away from home ties and sympathies, and of utter failure of the power of concentration. What is the key to the problem of the change that came over him in the first few years after his return ? The facts, on the surface, are sadly clear enough. Inherited tendencies to rheumatism and gout pursued Coleridge from boyhood. Indifference and carelessness as a schoolboy had tended to weaken his constitution. From his college days there are frequent references to ill-health in his letters, and, more ominous, to the depression that *constantly* came in its train. For the very keenness of his sensibilities was bound up with the close connection between his feelings and his intellect, and he always abandoned himself to the feelings of the moment. Increased ill-health, then, first, and accompanying depression, and secondly, opium, the fatal remedy, which he perhaps took occasionally as early as 1797, but which somewhere about this time became a regular resort in pain, till it grew to be his master, are facts which go far to account for the change.

To these must be added causes deep-rooted in Coleridge's peculiar temperament. This temperament he has analysed for us with characteristic naïveté in a description of himself to a correspondent whom he had not yet met : " As to me, my face, unless when animated by immediate eloquence, expresses great sloth, and great, indeed almost idiotic, good-nature. . . . As to my shape, 'tis a good shape enough if measured, but my gait is awkward, and the walk of the whole man indicates *indolence capable of energies*. . . . I compose very little, and I absolutely hate composition, and such is my dislike that even a sense of duty is sometimes too weak to overpower it."

It was he who described himself also as a great " tomorrower." This constitutional indolence often, moreover, found excuse and support for itself in the abstract speculations in which he loved to indulge. His mind, he told himself, was so " comprehensive in its conceptions " that it wasted itself " in the contemplation of the many things which it might do." And a long list, indeed, might be made of the numerous works which Coleridge proposed to himself and towards the execution of which he never put pen to paper ; though he possessed a marvellous faculty of deceiving himself into believing that one after another was on the verge of completion.

COLERIDGE & HIS POETRY

To these predisposing causes the habit of opium-taking came as a determining factor, and years of brilliant promise were succeeded by years of tantalising failure. But how far physical causes alone would have blighted achievement, how far the failure, at any rate of poetic power, was inevitable, it is impossible to decide. It is only possible to state the facts as they occurred.

In spite of real success as a journalist, early in 1800 Coleridge threw up his work for the "Morning Post." He did, however, before leaving London execute a translation of Schiller's "Wallenstein," which, though poorly received at the time, has since earned a deserved reputation.

He was unable to make up his mind to settle far from Wordsworth, and summer saw him established with his wife and children at Greta Hall, near Keswick, and within reach of Dove Cottage, with which a constant exchange of visits, like those between Alfoxden and Stowey, soon began. This year the second part of "Christabel" was written, but Coleridge was neither well nor happy. He sought refuge from himself in metaphysics, and in endless schemes of works he meant to undertake. He had "no heart for poetry," he wrote to Southey. "Alas ! alas ! how should I, who have passed eighteen months with giddy head, sick stomach, and swoln knees ? " The climate probably increased his rheumatism ; long expeditions over the mountains in all sorts of weather were taken, regardless of consequences. One of these, when Coleridge, " on the summit of Sca Fell," watched the effects of a thunderstorm among the mountains, gave rise to the following poem, which, however, owes much to a German original.

HYMN BEFORE SUNRISE, IN THE VALE OF CHAMOUNI

Hast thou a charm to stay the morning-star
In his steep course ?   So long he seems to pause
On thy bald awful head, O sovran BLANC !
The Arve and Arveiron at thy base
Rave ceaselessly ; but thou, most awful Form !
Risest from forth thy silent sea of pines,
How silently !   Around thee and above
Deep is the air and dark, substantial, black,
An ebon mass : methinks thou piercest it,
As with a wedge !   But when I look again,
It is thine own calm home, thy crystal shrine,
Thy habitation from eternity !
O dread and silent Mount ! I gazed upon thee,
Till thou, still present to the bodily sense,
Didst vanish from my thought : entranced in prayer
I worshipped the Invisible alone.

Yet, like some sweet beguiling melody,
So sweet, we know not we are listening to it,
Thou, the meanwhile, wast blending with my Thought,
Yea, with my Life and Life's own secret joy :
Till the dilating Soul, enrapt, transfused,
Into the mighty vision passing—there
As in her natural form, swelled vast to Heaven !

Awake, my soul ! not only passive praise
Thou owest ! not alone these swelling tears,

COLERIDGE & HIS POETRY

Mute thanks and secret ecstasy ! Awake,
Voice of sweet song ! Awake, my heart, awake !
Green vales and icy cliffs, all join my hymn.

Thou first and chief, sole sovereign of the Vale !
O struggling with the darkness all the night,
And visited all night by troops of stars,
Or when they climb the sky or when they sink :
Companion of the morning-star at dawn,
Thyself Earth's rosy star, and of the dawn
Co-herald : wake, O wake, and utter praise !
Who sank thy sunless pillars deep in Earth ?
Who fill'd thy countenance with rosy light ?
Who made thee parent of perpetual streams ?

And you, ye five wild torrents fiercely glad !
Who called you forth from night and utter death,
From dark and icy caverns called you forth,
Down those precipitous, black, jagged rocks,
For ever shattered and the same for ever ?
Who gave you your invulnerable life,
Your strength, your speed, your fury, and your joy,
Unceasing thunder and eternal foam ?
And who commanded (and the silence came),
Here let the billows stiffen, and have rest ?

Ye Ice-falls ! ye that from the mountain's brow
Adown enormous ravines slope amain—
Torrents, methinks, that heard a mighty voice,
And stopped at once amid their maddest plunge !
Motionless torrents ! silent cataracts !
Who made you glorious as the Gates of Heaven
Beneath the keen full moon ? Who bade the sun
Clothe you with rainbows ? Who, with living flowers
Of loveliest blue, spread garlands at your feet ?—

COLERIDGE & HIS POETRY

GOD ! let the torrents, like a shout of nations,
Answer ! and let the ice-plains echo, GOD !
GOD ! sing ye meadow-streams with gladsome voice !
Ye pine-groves, with your soft and soul-like sounds !
And they too have a voice, yon piles of snow,
And in their perilous fall shall thunder, GOD !

Ye living flowers that skirt the eternal frost !
Ye wild goats sporting round the eagle's nest !
Ye eagles, playmates of the mountain-storm !
Ye lightnings, the dread arrows of the clouds !
Ye signs and wonders of the element !
Utter forth God, and fill the hills with praise !

Thou too, hoar Mount ! with thy sky-pointing
      peaks,
Oft from whose feet the avalanche, unheard,
Shoots downward, glittering through the pure serene
Into the depth of clouds, that veil thy breast—
Thou too again, stupendous Mountain ! thou
That as I raise my head, awhile bowed low
In adoration, upward from thy base
Slow travelling with dim eyes suffused with tears,
Solemnly seemest, like a vapoury cloud,
To rise before me—Rise, O ever rise,
Rise like a cloud of incense from the Earth !
Thou kingly Spirit throned among the hills,
Thou dread ambassador from Earth to Heaven,
Great hierarch ! tell thou the silent sky,
And tell the stars, and tell yon rising sun
Earth, with her thousand voices, praises GOD.

Yet in spite of the fact that he could still joy
in Nature's splendours, that he delighted in
showing friends who visited Greta Hall the
beauties of the district, Coleridge was very
106

restless. He journeyed to London and Stowey ; the references in his letters to ill-health and depression, and to growing want of sympathy between himself and his wife, became more frequent. And to this growing sense of despair, coupled with the tragic conviction that was forcing itself upon him, that his poetic powers were dying, Coleridge gave saddest expression in the ode which has been called " the poet's dirge to his own imagination." It appeared under the title " Dejection : An Ode," in the " Morning Post " of October 4, 1802—the day when Wordsworth began a happy married life. In stanzas heavy with gloom, the poet describes the grief which has taken possession of him. No longer can he gain from Nature the joy she used to impart ; for he can no longer bring joy to meet her half-way ; and he has discovered, with Wordsworth, that she can give nothing to those who do not come ready to receive. Seldom has hopeless mood found such tragic utterance.

DEJECTION : AN ODE
I

Well ! If the Bard was weather-wise, who made
   The grand old ballad of Sir Patrick Spence,
   This night, so tranquil now, will not go hence
Unroused by winds, that ply a busier trade
Than those which mould yon cloud in lazy flakes,
Or the dull sobbing draft, that moans and rakes
     Upon the strings of this Æolian lute,
     Which better far were mute.

For lo ! the New-moon winter-bright !
And overspread with phantom light,
(With swimming phantom light o'erspread
But rimmed and circled by a silver thread)
I see the old Moon in her lap, foretelling
 The coming-on of rain and squally blast.
And oh ! that even now the gust were swelling,
  And the slant night-shower driving loud and
   fast !
Those sounds which oft have raised me, whilst they
  awed,
  And sent my soul abroad,
Might now perhaps their wonted impulse give,
Might startle this dull pain, and make it move and live !

II

A grief without a pang, void, dark, and drear,
 A stifled, drowsy, unimpassioned grief,
  Which finds no natural outlet, no relief,
   In word, or sigh, or tear—
O Lady ! in this wan and heartless mood,
To other thoughts by yonder throstle woo'd,
 All this long eve, so balmy and serene,
Have I been gazing on the western sky,
 And its peculiar tint of yellow green :
And still I gaze—and with how blank an eye !
And those thin clouds above, in flakes and bars,
That give away their motion to the stars ;
Those stars, that glide behind them or between,
Now sparkling, now bedimmed, but always seen :
Yon crescent Moon, as fixed as if it grew
In its own cloudless, starless lake of blue ;
I see them all so excellently fair,
I see, not feel, how beautiful they are !

COLERIDGE & HIS POETRY

III

My genial spirits fail ;
And what can these avail
To lift the smothering weight from off my breast ?
It were a vain endeavour,
Though I should gaze for ever
On that green light that lingers in the west :
I may not hope from outward forms to win
The passion and the life, whose fountains are within.

IV

O Lady ! we receive but what we give,
And in our life alone does Nature live :
Ours is her wedding-garment, ours her shroud !
And would we aught behold, of higher worth,
Than that inanimate cold world allowed
To the poor loveless ever-anxious crowd,
Ah ! from the soul itself must issue forth
A light, a glory, a fair luminous cloud
Enveloping the Earth—
And from the soul itself must there be sent
A sweet and potent voice, of its own birth,
Of all sweet sounds the life and element !

V

O pure of heart ! thou need'st not ask of me
What this strong music in the soul may be !
What, and wherein it doth exist,
This light, this glory, this fair luminous mist,
This beautiful and beauty-making power.
Joy, virtuous Lady ! Joy that ne'er was given,
Save to the pure, and in their purest hour,
Life, and Life's effluence, cloud at once and shower,
Joy, Lady ! is the spirit and the power,
Which wedding Nature to us gives in dower,

A new Earth and new Heaven,
Undreamt of by the sensual and the proud—
Joy is the sweet voice, Joy the luminous cloud—
    We in ourselves rejoice !
And thence flows all that charms or ear or sight,
  All melodies the echoes of that voice,
All colours a suffusion from that light.

VI

There was a time when, though my path was rough,
  This joy within me dallied with distress,
And all misfortunes were but as the stuff
  Whence Fancy made me dreams of happiness :
For Hope grew round me, like the twining vine,
And fruits, and foliage, not my own, seemed mine.
But now afflictions bow me down to earth :
Nor care I that they rob me of my mirth ;
    But oh ! each visitation
Suspends what nature gave me at my birth,
  My shaping spirit of Imagination.
For not to think of what I needs must feel,
  But to be still and patient, all I can ;
And haply by abstruse research to steal
    From my own nature all the natural man—
  This was my sole resource, my only plan :
Till that which suits a part infects the whole,
And now is almost grown the habit of my soul.

VII

Hence, viper thoughts, that coil around my mind,
    Reality's dark dream !
I turn from you, and listen to the wind,
  Which long has raved unnoticed.
      What a scream
Of agony by torture lengthened out
That lute sent forth ! Thou Wind, that rav st without,

Bare crag, or mountain-tairn, or blasted tree,
Or pine-grove whither woodman never clomb,
Or lonely house, long held the witches' home,
   Methinks were fitter instruments for thee,
Mad Lutanist ! who in this month of showers,
Of dark-brown gardens, and of peeping flowers,
Mak'st Devil's yule, with worse than wintry song,
The blossoms, buds, and timorous leaves among.
   Thou actor, perfect in all tragic sounds !
Thou mighty Poet, even to frenzy bold !
      What tell'st thou now about ?
      'Tis of the rushing of an host in rout,
   With groans of trampled men, with smarting
         wounds—
At once they groan with pain, and shudder with the cold!
But hush ! there is a pause of deepest silence !
   And all that noise, as of a rushing crowd,
With groans, and tremulous shudderings—all is over—
   It tells another tale, with sounds less deep and loud !
      A tale of less affright,
      And tempered with delight,
As Otway's self had framed the tender lay,
      'Tis of a little child
      Upon a lonesome wild,
Not far from home, but she hath lost her way :
And now moans low in bitter grief and fear,
And now screams loud, and hopes to make her mother
      hear.

VIII

'Tis midnight, but small thoughts have I of sleep :
Full seldom may my friend such vigils keep !
Visit her, gentle Sleep ! with wings of healing,
   And may this storm be but a mountain-birth,
May all the stars hang bright above her dwelling,
   Silent as though they watched the sleeping Earth !

With light heart may she rise,
   Gay fancy, cheerful eyes,
 Joy lift her spirit, joy attune her voice ;
To her may all things live, from pole to pole,
Their life the eddying of her living soul !
   O simple spirit, guided from above,
 Dear Lady ! friend devoutest of my choice,
Thus mayest thou ever, evermore rejoice.

A tour in Scotland, begun with the Wordsworths, from whom, however, he soon parted
on the score of ill-health, did nothing to mend
matters. It was while on this tour that he sent
home to Southey in a poem, " The Pains of
Sleep," a description of nights of agonising
torture—" a true portrait of my nights. What
to do, I am at a loss ; for it is hard thus to be
withered, having the faculties and attainments
which I have." What he did, at length, turned
out a fatal mistake. In the spring of 1804 he
set out for Malta, seeking health in a milder
climate. It seems practically beyond dispute
that there and in Italy, between 1804 and 1806,
his surrender to opium became complete.

VI

The story of the next twelve years must be
briefly told. It is a pitiful story enough, and
it has little to do with Coleridge as poet. On
his return to London he went first to Lamb,
with whom he had spent some time before
setting out. A visit paid to Wordsworth, who
was spending the winter at Coleorton, served

but to make him more fully conscious of the gulf between what might have been and what was. For here Wordsworth recited to him the " Prelude," an autobiographical record of full and harmonious development. It stirred Coleridge to the depths, and

Life's joy rekindling roused a throng of pains—

. . . . .

Sense of past youth, and manhood come in vain,
And genius given, and knowledge won in vain ;
And all which I had culled in wood-walks wild
And all which patient toil had reared, and all,
Commune with *thee* had opened out—but flowers
Strewed on my corse, and borne upon my bier,
In the same coffin, for the self-same grave.

A cry as pathetic as that in the " Ode to Dejection."

The next few years were years of wandering, uncompleted plans, and unrest. Coleridge visited his home, and went with Mrs. Coleridge and the children to Stowey and the west ; worked at irregular intervals for the " Courier " in London ; planned courses of lectures both in London and Bristol, some of which were delivered with his old brilliance, while others all the efforts of his friends could not keep either to the appointed date or the appointed subject. He projected, and while staying with the Wordsworths, at Keswick, actually published for some months, a periodical known as " The Friend," designed to make popular appeal, which had as its " main object " " to establish the philosophical distinction between the Reason and the Understanding.'' On its inevitable failure he left the Lake district.

It was while he was visiting in the west that De Quincey first met him and heard '' a continuous strain of eloquent dissertation '' lasting three hours.

Separation from Mrs. Coleridge was succeeded by gradual drifting away from many former friends, who often did not hear of him or know where he was for months. Constantly, indeed, he could not bring himself to open the letters he received. Most bitter of all was the estrangement from Wordsworth, caused by a mischief-making acquaintance, who repeated a remark made by Wordsworth in confidence. The breach was not healed for two years ; then a reconciliation took place, but things could never be again quite as they had been before. For a while there was a coolness, too, between him and Poole, and about this time, too, Josiah Wedgwood withdrew his share of the annuity. But Lamb remained ever faithful, and Coleridge's wonderful power of attracting new friends and of winning devotion never forsook him. During these years of unrest he found one friend after another willing and anxious to give him shelter, sympathy, and consolation. He spent much time with the Morgans at Hammersmith, whence he came up to give lectures at the London Philosophical Society, at which Byron was present. Of these, H. Crabb Robinson, friend of most of the literary men of the time, and henceforth friend and admirer of Coleridge, has given some account in his " Diary." Some were very brilliant ; some dull and rambling. The comments throw much light on the marvellous powers and characteristic failings of Coleridge's mind. One lecture is thus reported : "He was, by advertisement, to speak of 'Romeo and Juliet' and Shakespeare's females ; unhappily, some demon whispered the name of Lancaster in his ear ; and we had, in one evening, an attack on the poor Quaker, a defence of boarding-school flogging, a parallel between the ages of Elizabeth and Charles, a defence of what is untruly called unpoetic language, an account of the different languages of Europe, and a vindication of Shakespeare against the imputation of grossness ! ! ! . . . Yet it is lucky he has hitherto omitted no lecture. Living with the Morgans, they force him to come to the lecture-room, and this is a great point gained." Another lecture is described as " very desultory, again, at first, but when about half-way through he bethought himself of Shakespeare ; and though he forgot at last what we had been four times in succession to hear, viz., of Romeo and Juliet as lovers, yet he treated beautifully of 'The Tempest.' "

The following entry, referring to a lecture Coleridge delivered on " Hamlet," is of sinister significance :

" ' Action,' he said, ' is the great end of all ; no intellect, however grand, is valuable if it draw us from action and lead us to think and think till the time of action is passed by and we can do nothing.' Somebody said to me, ' This is a satire on himself.' ' No,' said I, ' it is an elegy.' A great many of his remarks on Hamlet were capable of a like application.''

Byron's admiration of his genius had practical effect in the acceptance of his '' Remorse,'' which had a successful run at Drury Lane. Two years later he roused himself to the production of a first instalment of '' Biographia Literaria,'' and was working at arranging poems for publication. Meanwhile Southey and others were caring for his wife and children, and it was left to them to make the effort necessary for sending Hartley to Oxford. With paralysed will, he seemed doomed to utter inability to respond to any '' moral obligation '' that had claim upon him. Realising his misery, he remained '' wretched, helpless and hopeless,'' as he described himself in a sad letter at the time. Yet deliverance awaited him. In April 1816, he at last made up his mind to take a step which he had long recognised as his only possible chance of self-conquest. He placed himself unreservedly in the hands of a physician, Dr. Gillman, of Highgate, in whose house and under whose affectionate care the rest of his life was passed.

COLERIDGE & HIS POETRY

The remainder of Coleridge's story is a record of gradual, remarkable emancipation from his fatal habit ; of kindly intercourse, renewal of old friendships, and formation of new ones ; and of steady, fruitful industry. It was not without its sorrows ; it could not be without its regrets. It was impossible that his old genius should come back to him as it had been before ; yet fragmentary gleams of his old power did come back to him ; and in other directions the work of his last years was among the most important of his life, though this, from the fact that it was so far-reaching, he probably could not himself realise.

The first work published after his arrival at Highgate was the unfinished "Christabel," which Murray had undertaken to print on Byron's recommendation. The critics received it hardly ; but the critics were behind the times. Since the publication of the "Lyrical Ballads" public taste had changed, and the poem had a large sale. Nevertheless, Murray published no more for him, and the failure of the publisher who produced his later works caused him serious loss, and involved him in a debt which was a source of worry—anxious as he now was to regain an independence for which all through his life he had cared too little.

Such stimulating and influential works as, in criticism, the "Biographia Literaria," and, in theology, the "Aids to Reflection" were published during these years. And in 1817 he issued the final collection of his poems published during his lifetime, under the title " Sibylline Leaves."

One of the most devoted of the friends who became attached to him during his closing years was Dr. J. H. Green, who was attracted to him through a common interest in metaphysics. To him was entrusted the compilation of the vast quantity of notes Coleridge left behind him, for the great work that was " to contain all knowledge and proclaim all philosophy," to the planning and dictation of which Coleridge, at Highgate, devoted so much of his time and energy.

It was Green who was walking with Coleridge in Highgate Lane when Keats met him and walked with him for two memorable miles, while he " broached a thousand things," from nightingales and poetry to ghosts, dreams, and metaphysics. " I heard his voice as it came towards me," wrote Keats. " I heard it as he moved away. I had heard it all the interval—if it may be called so."

The Gillmans not only did everything affection and sympathy could possibly suggest for their guest's comfort ; they made his friends as welcome as himself. Thither regularly came Lamb to visit him—Lamb, who found " either my eyes are grown dimmer or my old friend is the same who stood before me three-and-twenty years ago—his hair a little confessing the hand of time, but still shrouding the same capacious brain—his heart not altered, scarcely where it ' alteration finds.' " H. Crabb Robinson brought many literary men of note up to visit him. And thither, too, to the famous Thursday evening gatherings, which were a regular institution at Highgate from about 1824, came many a young enthusiast to listen to his golden eloquence—among the rest Julius Hare, John Sterling, and Thomas Carlyle, whose brilliant, though unsympathetic, picture of Coleridge as he then was, is famous. In his " Life of Sterling " he wrote :

" Coleridge sat on the brow of Highgate Hill in those years, looking down on London and its smoke and tumult, like a sage escaped from the inanity of life's battle ; attracting towards him the thoughts of innumerable brave souls still engaged there. . . . Here for hours would Coleridge talk concerning all conceivable or inconceivable things ; and liked nothing better than to have an intelligent or, failing that, even a silent and patient human listener. . . . To the man himself Nature had given in high measure the seeds of a noble endowment ; and to unfold it had been forbidden him. . . . Once more the tragic story of a high endowment with an insufficient will." Carlyle goes on to describe his appearance : " brow and head," massive and round ; " light hazel " eyes looking out on the world as in " mild astonishment " ; the rest of the face and figure " flabby and irresolute " and expressive of " weakness under possibility of strength." The dreaming, idealising " Prophet of Highgate Hill " had little in common with the " Sage of Chelsea."

Another friend of Coleridge's last years was his nephew and son-in-law, H. N. Coleridge, who afterwards edited the " Table Talk." It is thought to have been some temporary mis-understanding with him that gave rise to the depression in which Coleridge wrote the following exquisite little poem ; while he could write thus his hand had not lost its ancient cunning :

WORK WITHOUT HOPE

All Nature seems at work. Slugs leave their lair—
The bees are stirring—birds are on the wing—
And Winter slumbering in the open air,
Wears on his smiling face a dream of Spring !
And I the while, the sole unbusy thing,
Nor honey make, nor pair, nor build, nor sing.

Yet well I ken the banks where amaranths blow,
Have traced the fount whence streams of nectar flow.
Bloom, O ye amaranths ! bloom for whom ye may,
For me ye bloom not ! Glide, rich streams, away !
With lips unbrightened, wreathless brow, I stroll :
And would you learn the spells that drowse my soul ?
Work without Hope draws nectar in a sieve,
And Hope without an object cannot live.

Coleridge did not often leave the Gillmans for long. In 1828, however, he made a pleasant excursion with William and Dorothy Words-worth to the Rhine Valley. After that he went on no other distant journeys. The ill-health from which he had always suffered increased towards the close. Yet when the end came it came suddenly, and the last hours were free from pain. He died on July 25, 1834, in the house where he had found so peaceful a refuge after all his troubles. His grave is in Highgate Churchyard.

VIII

A correspondent of H. Crabb Robinson once wrote to him : " Of all men, there seems most need to say, ' God bless poor Coleridge ! ' One could almost believe that an enchanter's spell was upon him, forcing him to be what he is, and yet leaving him the power of showing what he might be." It is this tantalising feeling of unfulfilled possibilities that, in spite of Lamb's objection to the use of the adjective " poor " in connection with such a man, remains upper-most in our minds when we try to sum up our feelings about him. The tragedy of his wasted manhood is real enough and not to be mini-mised. It was one of those who knew him best who wrote, while aware of his achievements, " It vexes and grieves me to the heart that when he is gone . . . nobody will believe what a mind goes with him—how infinitely and ten-thousand-fold the mightiest of his genera-tion." Yet the sense of what he might have done must not be allowed to overshadow the realisa-tion of what he did. In the course of the story we have seen something of the great work that he and Wordsworth together accomplished for English poetry, freeing it from the trammels of eighteenth-century convention, and bringing to it once more genuine love of Nature and spiritual insight into her processes. Coleridge especially breathed into it afresh the spirit of high romance, wedded to modern knowledge of the "phenomena of mind." As a critic, among much else that is valuable, he gave Shakespeare back to the English people.

As a theologian, champion of orthodoxy as he grew conservative, he influenced greatly such rising men of the younger generation as F. D. Maurice, Kingsley, and Newman. He has been claimed as the teacher of greatest influence behind the Tractarian movement.

And the last note shall be personal. As a man he won and kept the love, admiration, and friendship of some of the noblest men of his generation. Nor let it be forgotten that against the "body that did him grievous wrong," after years of slavery and misery he rose up and conquered. This is not the least worthy of remembrance among his achievements.

Critics have compared the last years of quiet on Highgate Hill to the pale shining out of the sun before its setting. Rather would we say, wearied from the fight in the night of darkness that had engulfed him, Coleridge climbed to heights where, aloof from the struggle, with the violent ardours of youth left behind, yet with forward-looking thoughts, he spent what strength was left in brave endeavour to point others toward the sunrise.

BIBLIOGRAPHY

The following list contains the titles of a few books and essays which may be specially recommended for the further study of Coleridge and his work :

Traill, H. D. : "Coleridge" ("English Men of Letters").

Dykes-Campbell, J. : "Introduction" to the "Poetical Works" (also published separately).

Hall Caine : "Coleridge" ("Great Writers").

Shairp, J. C. : "Coleridge" in "Studies in Poetry and Philosophy."

Dowden, E. : "The French Revolution and English Literature."

Dowden, E. : "Coleridge as a Poet" in "New Studies in Literature."

Pater, W. : "Coleridge" in "Appreciations."

Coleridge's "Biographia Literaria."

Note.—Hall Caine's volume in the "Great Writers" series contains a very full bibliography.